Is God Fair (?)

And 22 Other Controversial
Biblical Interrogatories
Of Brother James

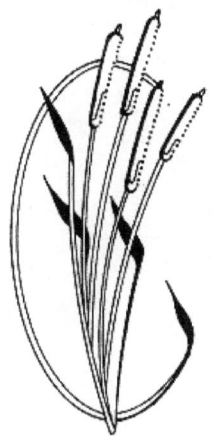

Is God Fair (?)
And 22 Other Controversial
Biblical Interrogatories
Of Brother James

Editors
Ray Glandon
Ravi Gurumoorthy

Cover Concept
Brother James

Backcover Artwork
Tim James

Senior Publisher
Steven Lawrence Hill Sr

A Publisher Trademark Title page

ASA Publishing Corporation
An Accredited Hybrid Publishing House with the BBB
(The Landmark Building)
23 E. Front St., Suite 103, Monroe, Michigan 48161
www.asapublishingcorporation.com

All Rights Reserved. No part of this publication may be reproduced, stored in a retrieval system or transmitted in any form or by any means electronic, mechanical, photocopying, recording or otherwise, without the prior written permission of the publisher. Author/writer rights to "Freedom of Speech" protected by and with the "1st Amendment" of the Constitution of the United States of America.

This is a work of non-fiction educational reference book and biblical knowledge. Any resemblance to actual events, locales, person living or deceased is entirely coincidental. Other names, places, and characters are within the work of historical/educational and biblical references.

Any and all vending sales and distribution not permitted without full book cover and this title page.

Copyrights©2017 Brother James, All Rights Reserved
Title: Is God Fair (?): And 22 Other Controversial Biblical Interrogatories of Brother James
Date Published: 07.09.2017
Edition: 1 *Trade Paperback*
Book ID: ASAPCID2380705
ISBN: 978-1-946746-08-5
Library of Congress Cataloging-in-Publication Data

This book was published in the United States
Great State of Michigan

A Publisher Trademark Copy page

DEDICATION

I sincerely dedicate this work of truth, as I see it, to the following:

My beloved late parents, Reverend Robert Walter James and his lovely wife, Juanita Mae Alexander James, who was the greatest teacher I ever met!

My extraordinarily spiritually, intellectually, and generous, gifted siblings who are blessing me daily: Robert Sylvester, William Richard, Dorcas Ann, Carolyn Lee, Timothy Allen, Frederick Louis and Alex Walter James and their progeny.

My Absolute Favorite Son, Oh, by the way, he is my ONLY Son, Hamadi Mugabe James.

My blood relations connected to the bloodlines of my late parents, too numerous to mention here as my family exercised the religious dictum, "Be fruitful and multiply."

The beacons of Truth in my life, some of whom I never met: Ralph Waldo "Petey Greene," Mwalimu Sundiata Keita, Kwame Ture (aka Stokely Carmichael), Angela Davis, Malcolm X, W.E. B. Dubois, Bill Maher of the HBO show, Real-time With Bill Maher, Pastor Donnie McClurkin (for taking a principled stand on 'Pimps in the Pulpit")

Ray Glandon for his extraordinary editorial input, "The Breakfast Club" of my beloved Barbershop – Dixon "University!"

My Homeboy, Muhammed Ali, "The Greatest Of All Time (GOAT)" for your unwavering faith in God and fearless and consistent execution of your principles.

Finally, I dedicate this nonfiction work of truth to all my teachers in life. Two of whom are worthy of note, Mrs. Webbie (1st grade) and Ms. Gilmore (6th grade) at James M. Bond Elementary School, Louisville, Kentucky.

In addition, I have always held the position that I thank Almighty God for all the people who love me and like me as well as all the people who hate me (Satan's entourage – my haters) and dislike me, because those who love and like me and hate and dislike me, love me and like me and hate me and dislike me, for the exact same reasons, that being, I am spiritual, intellectual, possess a sense of propriety and am exceedingly honest. Therefore, I thank God for all the people who love me and show it and all the people who do not love me and show it, because I have been truly blessed by both camps! I have learned how to treat and not how to mistreat others through my experiences with every person the Lord has blessed me to have intersected with me in my life. Those folks who love me and those who do not! I am an I John 3:18 kind of guy. The Apostle John wrote in the previously mentioned scripture, "^{18} Dear children, let us not love with words or speech but with actions and in truth (NIV)." I pray Almighty God will bless you, friend or adversary, or newfound friend or foe because the scripture teaches me, I am to accept you for who and what you are!

PREFACE

There is an oft quoted axiom that reads, "Repetition is the Mother of ALL learning!" So that my intent for writing this book is not widely misunderstood, I wish to state I do not hate all preachers; I do not hate all preachers; I do not hate all preachers! However, I do despise, detest, and deny the perverted teachings of those preachers who have both prostrated and prostituted themselves before the idol of filthy lucre, money! I refer to these alleged men and women of the cloth as charlatans of charisma and corruption, demagogues of demonic unrighteous deception, and most aptly, pimps in the pulpit.

I am not one to, in the proverbial sense, tar all preachers with the same brush, but I do realize that the Pareto Principle is in full effect in many houses of worship today.

Let me say clearly that there are some wonderful, dedicated, gifted, and truth teaching preachers in this country. However, as I just suggested, the Pareto Principle is in full effect because 80% of the truly ordained work of God is being accomplished by 20% of those who were called by God and not called to the ministry by themselves.

I have always held and promoted the belief that if people were to enter a pitch black darkened room and suddenly a small but bright light were to appear in the center of that room, witnesses to the light would be compelled to take one of three possible actions! First, they could choose to be drawn to the benefits of the light. Or, second, they could reject the light and exit its positive illuminating and impactful presence. Or, third, they could be so intimidated by the light, they would attempt to douse or extinguish the light.

If you are an intellectual with an innate sense of propriety, who listens intently to the voice of the Holy Spirit and are NOT arrogant, condescending, pompous, egomaniacal, braggadocios, and not given to putting others down because you are better read than they, then please feel free to consider yourself that light in the center of a darkened room. However, as my analogy would suggest, expect, that when you come into the presence of ungodly people whose intellect, spirituality, and moral standing is diametrically opposed to yours, they will try to block or extinguish your light. The people of this ilk are covered in the darkness of values taken from Reality TV Shows, popular gossip magazines, and the inane and insane dribble of social media on the Internet. Please allow me to pause here and agree with that great American social commentator, the Mark Twain of our day, . . . Charles Barkley, "the Internet (social media) is the place where 'losers' go to make themselves FEEL important by criticizing others." Those who live in darkness hate on spiritual, intellectual, and moral people. These spiritually, morally, and intellectually allergic folks are passionate contributors to idle and inane gossip as what was referred to in my childhood as "Who Shot John." So, if you are the light in a darkened room, please do not become dismayed when only a few people are drawn to your worldview, your light. Know that others, whom I respectfully suggest to you, will be in the majority, and will make every concerted attempt to embarrass, humiliate, and attempt to destroy you. These misguided haters, whom Karl Marx labelled as the lumpen proletariat, will attempt to destroy you by telling others that you are a "Know It All."

Rest assured that those who may consider you a "know it all" probably have not read a book of any relevance and significance since high school. These lumpen, allergic to proper English, and anti- dictionary folk, will be intimated by you! So, expect them to endeavor to castigate and denigrate you in the presence of others.

But enough of my rantings of those who do not live by the African Proverb, "Not to know is BAD. Not to wish to know is WORSE!" This proverb is especially true when we consider our real knowledge of God's Word. I know people who read the Bible every day, but reading the Bible without other tools, such as a Bible Dictionary, a Concordance, or a Commentary to aid in your understanding of God's Word is merely reading the Bible. I repeat, reading the Bible without any biblical study tools is merely reading the Bible! And if your pastor discourages you from owning a Commentary, insisting that commentaries are written by man, then please politely ask him or her to explain the difference between a Commentary and a sermon!

Hence, this book, my new friend, is designed to open our eyes to some teachings I firmly believe make the Lord unhappy. It is my belief that what we believe about God's Word and our total reliance on some man or woman to properly interpret same without our doing our due diligence displeases God.

I believe the Lord expects us to verify the true meaning of His Word for ourselves.

We should strive to know the Word of God as well as we know the activities of celebrities, entertainers, sports figures, etc. We should be as addicted to the Word of God as a crack cocaine abuser is addicted to that dreaded drug that requires a hit with great frequency. My analogy suggests we might want to go into God's House as often as a crack addict enters a crack house! We should have a yearning for the learning of correct Christian principles and implement them every day of our lives.

To leave our salvation in the hands of some greedy man or woman who may be a charlatan and a minuscule anti-Christ makes as much sense as to come into a fortune and bury it in the backyard, expecting to one day in the distant future dig it up and find some accumulated interest.

I may not know you, but I know that you are capable in most instances to know when you hear something that is "too good to be true."

I wrote this book to open a serious dialogue as to what we believe and why we believe it! Hitler's Minister of Propaganda, Dr. Joseph Goebbels, said, "Repeat a lie a thousand times and it becomes the truth!" Do you know the lie of the prosperity gospel? Paul said in Galatians 1:6-7 (NIV) [6]I am astonished that you are so quickly deserting the one who called you to live in the grace of Christ and are turning to a different gospel—[7]which is really no gospel at all. Evidently some people are throwing you into confusion and are trying to pervert the gospel of Christ.

Do you attend a church where you are told the King James Version of the Bible is the ONLY true version of the Bible? Well, guess what? The current version of the KJV is a translation of the original version of the Bible published in 1611, and it was and still is known as the "Authorized King James Version!" Hmm, it seems what Goebbels said has merit as it relates to what we hear espoused from the pulpits in this country!

My intent is to ask you some challenging questions about your beliefs so you might gauge whether you are spiritually being led to slaughter by a Judas goat! I pray that you are not financially supporting someone who will die materialistically rich off the fruits of your labor. I do not know what they call this type of practice where you live, but in the neighborhood I grew up in, it's called "pimping."

The choice we all need to make in life is whether to serve God or man. If we chose to serve man, are we the tricks/Johns (procurers of the services of a prostitute) or the prostitutes? There are too many preachers who are pimping their congregants with the prosperity and plant-a- seed false gospels. And guess who is getting RICH?

Prayerfully and hopefully you will not imbibe the poisoned Kool Aid taught in many churches in this Country. I sincerely pray that by researching the lessons contained herein, you will learn to discern and reach your own truth.

May Almighty God bless you on this journey into what I believe to be unchartered spiritual waters. Should anyone be offended by what appears herein and also feel the need to denigrate and castigate my character, please be reminded of another oft quoted axiom, "When a rock is thrown into a pack of wolves, only the one that is hit yelps!"

Table of Contents

Dedication .... (a)

Preface .... (i)

ARTICLE 1
Are You A PK Who Is Tired Of Being Held to a Different Christian Standard?..1

ARTICLE 2
At What Age Should a Child Be Baptized? 6

ARTICLE 3
Do You Really Believe There is a Place Called Heaven?........18

ARTICLE 4
What Kind of Student of God's Word Are You? 21

ARTICLE 5
Do You Have an Awe Inspiring Testimony? Looking for Lena Horne: How The Lord Comforted Me While I was Temporarily Blind 26

ARTICLE 6
What Would You Do If You Were Jesus For A Day?..............29

ARTICLE 7
Is God Always Fair, and Does He Have to Be? 36

ARTICLE 8
Are You a Punk Ass Christian?...47

ARTICLE 9
Did God Call You To Sit On The Bench? 57

ARTICLE 10
Is it a Sin for Christians to Drink Alcohol? 62

ARTICLE 11
Are You a Re-Gifting Christian? 71

ARTICLE 12
Are You on God's Team or Satan's Team? 75

ARTICLE 13
Do You Realize Who You Have in Your Corner When in A the Heated Battle Against Satan? 82

ARTICLE 14
Are You Willing to Forfeit Your Life for a Godly Cause? 87

ARTICLE 15
Are You a Spoiled Christian? 91

ARTICLE 16
Will God Allow You to Enter The Gates of Heaven with a "D" Average? 95

ARTICLE 17
Are You Going THROUGH Something? 99

ARTICLE 18
Are You a SINgle, Saved, and Satisfied Christian? 112

ARTICLE 19
Does Your Pastor Meet The Biblical Criteria Of an Effective Spiritual Leader? 123

ARTICLE 20
Do You Aspire To Be A Church Celebrity? 132

ARTICLE 21
Do You TRULY Understand What You Are Doing When You Say,... AMEN? 139

ARTICLE 22
Are You A SUCKA For A Pimp In The Pulpit? 143

ARTICLE 23
Do You Want and Need a God You Can See? 164

EPILOGUE 169
Book Credits 173

Is God Fair (?)

And 22 Other Controversial
Biblical Interrogatories
Of Brother James

ARTICLE 1

Are You a PK Who Is Tired of Being Held to a Different Christian Standard?

I am a PK, a Preacher's Kid. I am the second eldest of eight children, born to the late Reverend Robert W. James and his lovely wife Juanita M. A. James. My father's church was located 132 miles away from our home in Louisville, Kentucky. Weather permitting, the entire family made that long and arduous trip for many Sunday's during my childhood. I say all this to convey that my parents were working class poor folks, and as far as I can remember, my father never drove a fancy car or made a lot of money as a preacher and certainly did not live in a fine, well-appointed home. We lived in abject poverty until each of my siblings and I were able to make it in the world on our own.

Why is this important? Well, when people hear you are a PK, they automatically and incorrectly assume you are part of the middle class, an elite member of the socio-economic milieu, that you attended the best private schools and universities, and vacationed in the Caribbean or some European capitol every year. Nothing was farther from the truth. We never lived the lifestyle of the rich and famous. Some people still had a tendency to treat us differently from our "Christian" peers. Our peers often teased us to the extreme and typically would try to entice us into some sin, they were well versed in just so they could have the Associated Press or Reuther's News Service report our misdeeds to the world.

As a PK, I grew up resenting the fact that people treated me differently only because my father was a preacher and I was his son. I would often tell people that God called my father to preach, not his entire family too.

One of my fondest stories I tell to illustrate this point is where I was about 10 years old. Neighborhood boys and I were playing "stick ball" in the street on the block I lived on. It is important that you understand that I was playing stick ball while many of the parents were watching. All of a sudden I heard a loud and highly irritated voice that I can still hear today say, "Henry, what are you doing? Why aren't you in your house reading your Bible? After all, you are a Reverend James's son!" It was all I could do to restrain my response, which would have been very disrespectful. However, that was a different day, when children did not talk back to adults. I restrained my response until I calmed myself, then politely responded, "My parents want us to get some exercise like the rest of the kids." You see, the lady who chastised me, had not one, but two sons playing stick ball. They had been baptized, so why should they be allowed on that day to play while I was expected to go in the house to pray and read my Bible. I found myself resenting the stigma heaped upon me just because my father was a preacher. This twisted mindset would continue to follow me for the rest of my life.

I can remember many instances where people would have events and a friend would invite me to hang out with them at the event, but when I entered the premises, the James Brown song being played would abruptly stop. The glasses of liquor or bottles of beer would disappear. The festive mood that was obvious and permeating the room immediately dissipated and devolved to the solemn and mournful atmosphere of a wake. On one particular occasion the person who invited me was called into another room of the house where the party was being held. He was grilled as if he had committed a serious criminal offense. "What the hell is the matter with you, bringing Reverend James's son here while we are trying to have a good time?"

I would question why some people think that Christians are not supposed to have fun listening to secular music, playing cards, engaging in the latest dance craze, and having a cool drink of the beverage of their choice all in the name of fun? Why was my being a PK perceived as a plague or a curse by those who would be sitting in a pew on Sunday afternoon? Being a PK is a tough task, one I do not wish upon anyone who has to deal with those folks who would treat them as a social pariah! I often find myself pondering why, when Christians are talking about sports, or music, or current events, they are shocked about my knowledge of these and other topics! I remember teaching Sunday School and using the lyrics of the artist TI, or Common, or Talib Kweli, or Floetry, to reinforce a point to the utter amazement of the participants. The usual remark was, "How do you know about...?" Being the extremely polite person that I am, I replied, "I know about them the same way you do. I listen to their music."

This deferential treatment followed me into adult life. I love to pray now, but in years past, I dreaded being at an occasion where there was a meal and someone would say, without asking me in advance, "and now we will have a Reverend James's son bless the food!" I would sometimes ask why I had to be the one, and the answer would always be, "because you are the preacher's son!" Oh yes, let me not forget those people who attended a funeral alongside me, and when the Home Going Service allowed for two minute remarks, people who knew dearly departed better and longer than I would ask me, "Hey, why don't you go up and say something on our behalf!" "Why me," I would abruptly ask? "Why not you," they would respond or should I say, retort. "After all, you are a preacher's son!"

We should all be ready and know how to pray at an event. We need to carry ourselves in a respectful, kind, and Christian manner. We should live a life that is intended to be Christ-like so we might enter the gates of heaven. We should never fear being ostracized at the lunch table if we bless our food before our peers. We would not allow ourselves to live with the double standard that has unfairly imposed upon the PK's of the world or should I say the Christian world. Why should the PK's be treated any differently than other Christians? After all, God calls the preacher to lead his or her designated flocks, not his entire family!

While some may have been incorrectly taught or may just assume based upon their experiences here on earth, let me assure you that there are no VIP sections in heaven for preachers, deacons, trustees, ministry heads, and most importantly, to me or any PK's! Each and every person, believers and non-believers alike, will one day have to answer for every thought, word, and deed, whether good or bad. We must all pay a price before we enter heaven.

I envision heaven as a place where everyone will be part of a constant chorus singing praises to God. There will be no choir directors, no lead singers, and no discords in the heavenly choir. Everyone will have an equal part on God's team, and everyone will play an equal role. So do not think that your pastor or even you will be seated at a special table in heaven. No, we will all be equal in God's eyes, so why would we not be equal down here on earth?

As a PK, I have no special role to play in building God's

kingdom. My role is no greater than yours as we are all God's sons and daughters. So, please STOP putting more responsibility on the PK's in your life than you have placed or accepted in your own life. Please treat them as you want to be treated. After all, isn't that what God expects of us all? To love our neighbors as ourselves readily implies that we should treat our neighbors as we would want to be treated. I feel certain without having met you that you, would NOT want to be ostracized, criticized, and have unfair levels of responsibility heaped upon you like that heaped upon us PK's just because one or both of our parents are preachers! With the concept of all things being EQUAL, my posture on this issue is only fair, don't you think?

ARTICLE 2

At What Age Should a Child Be Baptized?

How old were you when you came to Christ? Were you overcome with an awe-inspiring and indescribable feeling of joy, excitement, and contentment that led you to leave your seat and walk down the aisle of a church to accept the religious leader's invitation to Discipleship? I am referring to that segment of a worship service where the pastor, elder, apostle, bishop, etc. opened the doors of the church. Or, were you in the privacy of your home where you may have even fallen to your knees but knew without any further deliberation that you needed Jesus in your life? It is of great import that I politely and respectfully ask you what led to your decision to accept Jesus Christ, Jesus of Nazareth, Jesus the Son of God as your personal Lord and Savior.

Throughout the years when the invitation for discipleship has been announced, I have borne witness to several children as young as six years old deliberately walking to the front of the church to accept Jesus Christ as their Lord and Savior. Most made this journey pensively at the urging of their parents. The parents' obvious pride and extreme joy in their child's act of faith, provoked or not, was readily apparent.

I have some excellent recollections where tears of joy profusely streamed down the parents' faces. Oh, what a glorious day. I assumed they thought their child believes in

Jesus.

Romans 10:9 (If you declare with your mouth, "Jesus is Lord," and believe in your heart that God raised him from the dead, you will be saved. NIV) informs us that all anyone needs to do is confess with their lips that they believe in Jesus, His death and Divine resurrection, and accept Him as their personal Lord and Savior, and they will therefore, be entitled to enter heaven. That is a monumental amount of data for anyone to absorb and fully understand at an early age!

But my question has always been in which Jesus does these very young converts truly know and believe? Which Jesus have they experienced and accepted as their Lord and Savior? Is it the Spiritual Jesus or the Historical Jesus upon which they are basing their salvation and eternal life? In my mind, one must have full knowledge or, should I say, at the very least, a rudimentary knowledge of each Jesus we have been introduced to in our lives.

As a child, my siblings and I were raised in a very religious household. Our father was a Baptist preacher and our mother was a gifted Sunday School teacher who also played piano. We were taught all the stories of Jesus' life, such as His teaching the elders in the Temple when He was only twelve years old. When one adds to that the story of Jesus feeding the multitude with five fish and five barley loaves of bread, the raising of Lazarus from the dead, His walking on water, etc., we could not help but believe the greatness of this truly gifted and inspiring man. And, of course, we obviously considered the source of these stories, our parents!

I recall the stories of Jesus, my parents and other adults in church shared with me in Sunday School, Baptist Training Union (BTU), and let us not forget Vacation Bible School. Was I being taught the Historical Jesus, the Spiritual

Jesus, or both? And can we be taught the truth of the Spiritual Jesus, or must we experience the Spiritual Jesus for ourselves? Did I fully understand what it means to have Jesus in my life? Could I, as a child, fully explain to one of my peers what Jesus meant to me and should mean to them? No, I could not because all I could do was relate stories about Jesus gleaned from the teachings of adults who lied to me about the Tooth Fairy, Easter Bunny, Santa Claus, etc.

Were these blatantly malicious lies about mythical figures intended to harm me and other children? Were there some insidious plots to keep children focused on the ever-present materialism in our society? Yes, I said these myths were capitalistic and materialistic in nature as they all promised the recipient some form of a gift! Think about that for a minute. The myths of the Tooth Fairy, Easter Bunny, and Santa Claus all promised some type of gift or gifts, but God promises us a tremendous, incomparable gift in the form of His Son, Jesus Christ?

Please, go ahead and marinate on my question for a few minutes. I will wait as I have time!

No, the rationale for these myths (primarily derived from pagan practices) was designed to give children, at the very least, a degree of HOPE! I was startled while doing my research for this article to find that some psychologists see no harm in teaching children these myths of the Tooth Fairy, Easter Bunny, and Santa Claus. But, is it correct and righteous to teach children lies at an early age to provide them with a positive future outlook, a sense of HOPE? Would the words and teachings of Jesus not be sufficient instead of the promise of money left on a pillow, collecting a bunch of dyed boiled eggs, or a bevy of gifts brought down the chimney by obese Jolly St. Nick? These myths linger in the recesses of my mind to this very day, and they lay the foundation to what I allude to when I refer to the Historical Jesus. By the way, we did not have a chimney in the house I grew up in, but my siblings and I still waited to see if any gifts were left by Santa Claus on Christmas morning! Does not the Spiritual Jesus offer us HOPE through our faith in Him? Hebrews 11:1 in the NIV translation of the Bible may help our understanding where it states, "Now faith is confidence in what we <u>hope</u> for and assurance about what we do not see." Hmm, how many 6–8 year olds do you know who could explain their belief in Jesus as it relates to their hope and faith? How many young folks could explain in a simple way the basis of their faith and their hope of seeing Jesus in heaven? How many 6-8 year olds could readily explain the often espoused statement, "knowledge of the word brings about faith. Faith brings about obedience and obedience brings about good works!" I am not saying these children do not believe in Jesus. My question is which one?

I am not mad at my late parents and others who taught me the aforementioned myths, but my point is, if I could easily believe in these myths and mythical figures and learn later in life they were not real, how deeply spiritual and sincerely reverentially oriented could my understanding of Jesus be? I did not question my knowledge of the Tooth Fairy, Easter Bunny, and Santa Claus whose gifts I could see. Is it possible I did not put the appropriate energy into my understanding of the gifts of Jesus, whose gifts of salvation and eternal life I could neither see nor appreciate at an early age?

But to whom is the Spiritual Jesus, I alluded?

To have a better understanding of the Spiritual Jesus, we must look at the factors that must be clearly understood to combine an understanding of the Historical and Spiritual Jesus. There are at least two prohibitive factors I believe that prevent young children from understanding and differentiating the "Spiritual" Jesus from the "Historical" Jesus. I feel we must look at Jesus from two distinct perspectives. First, we must look at the wisdom of Jesus that He imparted to the illiterate masses through His parables. Second, and most importantly, we should share our testimony or testimonies of the Spiritual Jesus simply through our individual experiences with Him! Our experiences with the Spiritual Jesus should lead us to Him and guide us to try to emulate and model His pristine, sin free, and incorruptible life.

I offer as evidence the wisdom of Jesus via his use of 46 parables. These parables used simplistic imagery equivalent to the icons for the copy, cut and paste, and print functions on our computers today. The messages within the parables of Jesus were easily understood by the people of His day, no matter their status in society.

I find it difficult to comprehend how a child might understand the meaning of Jesus' parables when many adults obviously do not today. Need an example? The parable of sowing a seed has absolutely nothing to do with money. If you did not hear me, the parable of the sower of the seed was about sowing a "spiritual SEED" not a monetary one! Shame on you pastors, bishops, apostles, elders, etc. who teach this exploitative and false meaning of the true meaning of God's Word! But I digress, and I will explain my unequivocal assentation on the "you must sow a seed" false doctrine in another article within this work! I will state categorically, as I depart from this point, that the planting of a monetary seed is UTTER NONSENSE!

I love all the parables of Jesus, but there are two that stand out in my mind: the parable of the five talents found in Matthew 25:14-30 and the parable of the clean house found in Matthew 12:43-45. But what is a parable?

A parable was a simple and easily remembered story that Jesus used to deliver His fundamental Christian teachings. The parables of Jesus always had a singular message that used language and images that were readily understood by all who heard them. The parable of the 5 talents teaches us three undeniable points. First, God will hold each of us accountable for using the gifts, no matter how great or small He has bestowed upon us to build His heavenly kingdom. Second, this parable also teaches us to work diligently for the Lord at all times because He is our Lord and Master. He is our provider, protector, and we are to work for Him as opposed to our own egocentric interest. Third, the parable of the five talents teaches us that our success in life will be based upon our serious and dedicated efforts to serve God, not man. Yes, there are those we see who deny and are inimical to God and who appear to be beyond successful. However, we have something they do not possess and possibly never will, Jesus, as our GPS to heaven! Additionally, Kevin Hart has a mantra he and his crew recite just before he does a live stage performance. Kevin Hart, as I understand, assembles his crew and prays in a circle. He then gets ready for his live comedy performance by chanting, "Everybody wants to be famous, but everybody does not want to put the work in!" Thanks, Kevin Hart, for making my point about this parable. There were three servants, two of which blessed their master by putting the work in! The master blessed them according to how he had been blessed by their efforts. The third servant was lazy and lacked initiative, but felt he was equally entitled to be blessed by his master, even though he did not put the work in. The master is the representative of God, and we are the servants in this parable. What kind of servant of God are you? Do you put the necessary work in to be successful in God's vineyard? Oh, by the way, do you think a 6-8 year old child could explain the plain and simple message of this parable to one of their peers?

I previously mentioned that when the doors of the church are opened, it is known as a call to discipleship. I have come to understand that the word disciple has a threefold meaning: one who spreads the doctrine of someone else, student, and recruiter. That being said, can a 6–8 year old child be a student of the Gospel of Jesus Christ? Yes! Can they spread the Gospel of Jesus Christ to others? Possibly, but on a limited basis, they could only share with others the stories of the Historical Jesus. Can they also be recruiters of nonbelievers into God's kingdom? I am not sure! May I ask at this juncture, at what age should a child be baptized, if upon being baptized, they are expected to work in God's vineyard?

The third servant in the parable of the five talents wanted to be equally blessed by his master, but he simply did not put the work in! Do you feel a child could easily recognize the simplicity of Jesus' message in this parable? I think not. But let us continue.

My second favorite parable is the parable of the clean house. In this parable Jesus teaches us to always be vigilant once we become Christians because those issues in life that we forsake to become Christians might make us question His power, and His omnipresence will intensify after we accept Him as our Lord and Savior. What are some of the reasons you did not go to church after accepting Jesus? Were you offered overtime on a Sunday and opted to make that money instead of going to church? Were you in a relationship that dissolved because of something you did to cause the breakup? Did you miss the weekly Bible Study and / or church because you went back to the Club to find that special someone? Does a child know in times of trials and tribulations to turn to Jesus for a positive resolution? Does a child know that Jesus is an on time Lord and may not answer their prayers as quickly as the Tooth

Fairy, Easter Bunny, and Santa Claus? Do we or children know to lean on Jesus as opposed to our own understanding to fix our adverse situation in troubled times? Does a child understand that Jesus is the ultimate doctor if we are ill? Do children realize they should call on the name of Jesus when they are being bullied in school, or do they call upon their big brother or sister instead?

    I ask this litany of questions as we look at the parable of the clean house. The clean house is emblematic of our Christian lives where Jesus has washed away our sins, washed us CLEAN! When we accept Jesus, we should become a clean house. Do you remember the scripture that suggests that our bodies are a temple? There was a demon in a house, but when the owner of the house became saved, the demon lost total control of the new believer. Being determined to regain his influence over the new believer, the demon gathered seven other demons to invade the clean house. One plus seven is eight, and the Biblical significance of the number eight is that it is God's number of New Birth, New Beginning, and a New Creation. Seven is God's number of <u>Spiritual</u> Completion and Perfection! So, when we become a new creation in Jesus Christ, we should expect to be attacked by the demons of lying, jealousy, anger, temptation to do evil, the love of money, lust, immorality, and unwarranted acts of persecution. These are all concepts only a mature Christian should understand. Can a child who believes in the Tooth Fairy, Easter Bunny, and Santa Claus grasp this spiritual concept? Could a 6–8 year old believer understand and explain the nuances within Jesus' parable of the clean house with their peers? I sincerely think not!

    The second portion of my thesis about the Spiritual Jesus is that many of us had to meet Jesus through some profound and sometimes earth shaking experience. Yes, I was raised in a Christian household by a preacher and his incredibly devout wife. Yes, I believed in the Historical Jesus for many years after my baptism at eleven years of age. However, I came to understand that I had to truly experience the power of Jesus in my life for myself!

<u>Back in 1972 I was living in Columbus,</u> Ohio. For all intents and purposes I was a relatively healthy person. Then one day I began to have serious problems ingesting and digesting solid food and fluids. I consulted an internist who suggested I see a gastroenterologist. This doctor examined me and discovered that I had cysts and polyps in my throat and esophagus. These growths required surgery for removal. My surgery was scheduled for early in the morning. Admittedly, when I went to the hospital the night before the surgery, I was extremely nervous! This was the first of many serious surgeries I was to endure in my life! I could not sleep the night before my surgery. I also must admit that I was deserving of the Back Slider of the Year Award as a result of my minimal church attendance. However, I still prayed all night long just like Jesus did in the garden the night He was apprehended by the Jewish guards who turned Him over to the Romans for trial and execution. Why me, Lord? Why me, I asked in my most fervent prayers. Early the next morning the anesthesiologist visited me to insure me all would be well in regards to my surgery. Then the physician scheduled to perform the surgery entered the room. He also comforted me and assured me I had nothing to worry about. He then inserted a small hand held scope down my throat to perform one last check of the cysts and polyps clogging my digestive tract. He stepped back after the primary investigation of my throat and looked extremely puzzled, much to my consternation! The physician stepped back and examined the scope as if it was malfunctioning, and looked at my throat a second and third time. I will never forget the amazed look on

his face.

"Mr. James, you might as well get dressed because I will not be operating on you today," the doctor said in a highly mystified tone.

My heart began to race as a car at the Indy 500! Oh my God, I am dying, and there is nothing any surgery can do for me, I thought! Tears began to well up in my eyes when the doctor said astonishingly, "Mr. James, I do not know what to say, but all the growths in your throat are GONE! I have no explanation, but to suggest that it is a MIRACLE!" At that very moment, I knew there was a Spiritual Jesus who had answered my prayers. It was the Spiritual Jesus, not a Historical Jesus, that loved me so much He decided to operate on me while I could not sleep and removed the cysts and polyps in my digestive tract without any scalpels or anesthesia. This miracle bolstered my faith, and it was not the last miracle Jesus performed in my life! My faith in Him has never wavered since.

This is when I met the Spiritual Jesus. It was He, who, accompanied by the Holy Spirit, came into my life and became more than a Historical and mythical figure to me. This experience with the Spiritual Jesus clearly illustrated for me that while I thought I formerly knew Jesus and sometimes questioned His love for me, I knew Him from the standpoint of His Grace, His Power, and His Mercy. All of these traits were ever-present in my life, but I was looking at them from an improper vantage point! Could a child facing adversity properly come to a similar conclusion differentiating the Historical Jesus from the Spiritual Jesus? In the eloquent words of former NBA superstar, Charles Barkley, "I could be wrong, but I don't think so!"

So, I am not knocking those of you who were baptized

at an early age. That was a good thing because you at least had a concept of Jesus. I suggest to you, until you meet Jesus through His answering your most difficult needs, you just might not be acquainted with both the Historical and the Spiritual Jesus.

Do you have a testimony you could relate as to how Jesus was right on time with a major blessing in your life? Could you tell others why they should believe in Jesus using yourself as an example? Has Jesus brought you through your trials and tribulations as He did as His Father's servant, His devout servant JOB? If you answered yes, then I respectfully suggest you have made a connection with the Spiritual Jesus.

I am an Anabaptist. Anabaptists do not believe in baptisms at birth. They believe every believer should know the real Jesus and what He is doing in their lives.

So, at what age should a child be urged to accept Jesus as their Lord and Savior? Which Jesus do you know and believe in? Do you know and believe in the Historical Jesus or do you know the Spiritual Jesus who along with God the Father and the Holy Spirit have blessed you throughout your life? Did I give you something to think about as it relates to, what age should a child be baptized?

I respectfully offer the following test for parents to gauge whether or not your child knows both the Historical and Spiritual Jesus. Ask your child, "Do you believe in Jesus? Do you want to be baptized?" If they answer "yes" to both questions, then ask, "Do you believe in Santa Claus, the Easter Bunny, and the Tooth Fairy?" If their answer is again a resounding "YES" maybe, you might want to wait to rush them to be baptized. Maybe they are not truly ready to be baptized.

Please stay blessed as you strive to increase your knowledge of God's Word. The future of Christianity is at stake!

ARTICLE 3

Do You Really Believe There is a Place Called Heaven?

Do you truly believe in a place called heaven? Do you believe in paradise or a utopian metaphysical society in the clouds? Do you really believe you will see and be reunited with all those loved ones who made their transition before you to another place, another realm, a spiritual as opposed to a physical or earthly plane that we have yet to see in our lives? If your answer is YES, then why do we say some inane, inappropriate, and let me be blunt, ungodly, nonspiritual and Biblically incorrect things in a sad and a feeble attempt to comfort those we know have a loved one that made their transition to heaven? Why do we express at wakes and Home Going Services the sentiment, "I am sorry for your LOSS!"

On September 9, 2015, one of my Best or as we say in the Detroit area, BESTEST and Dearest friends in the Whole Wide World, Donell Green, made his transition. His passing after a bout with pneumonia was unexpected, and I hollered. I mean I HOLLERED when I received the call informing me that he was gone!

Donell made his transition at the chronologically young age of 59! Donell is my HERO! Why, because Donell is an excellent example, or should I say he is the epitome and an icon of a good son, a good brother, a good uncle, a good cousin, a good husband, a good father, a good stepfather and step grandfather, a good friend, a good neighbor, a good fellow congregant, and most importantly and tantamount to all his gifts, he is a good Christian. He knows the Word of God and easily shared the Word with adults and youth alike with equal aplomb. We were co-teachers of God's Word, and he remains a perfect role model for young Christian men.

I truly thank God for allowing me to be blessed to know this very unique and truly devoted Christian man, a man I love like a brother. I love him for the things he did for me and will from now on, love him for traits such as being so intuitive that he is always there when I need him. He is always there when I need someone to provide me with excellent Christian counsel on varied subjects and situations. He is there when I stubbornly want to do things my way, but reminds me to be patient and do things God's way! And I especially love him for the things he did not do! Donell never spoke ill of me. He never lied to me. He never got angry or was impatient with me. He was never pretentious or condescending to me, and most importantly, he never, ever treated me in an unchristian- manner. If you were to check with any of his myriad family members and friends, I am sure they would share this sentiment with anyone.

So please, do me a favor and stop telling people who have loved ones who have passed away, "I am sorry for your loss!"

If we truly believe in eternal life, and if we truly believe in Heaven, then that loved one is not lost. We can never, ever lose anyone or anything if we know exactly where they are or where it is!

I adamantly refuse to speak in the past tense of Donell, my parents, or any other loved ones who the Lord called to make their transition. They live within me as a direct result of their non-pareiled Christian love and influence demonstrated to me throughout the blessed times we spent together. My friend, Donell, is neither a loss to me nor to his family and friends because I know and we know exactly where he is and the company he is keeping.

So again, I beg and implore you to never speak of those we love who have made their transition in terms of "a Loss." We have not lost them because we are assured they are with the Lord in Heaven, and we should do as God's Word stipulates so we WILL one day see them again!

Just something for us to think about if we truly believe in Heaven!

ARTICLE 4

What Kind of Student of God's Word Are You???

Too many Christians feel that by simply reading the Word of God and then praying for His guidance, they have put forth appropriate effort of study to have a complete and total understanding of God's Holy Word. I tend to differ with this point of view. I see this posture as a major spiritual fallacy leading to some incorrect interpretations of our Christian beliefs. I firmly believe most Christians do not have the proper tools to accurately study God's Word so they might not, as Proverbs 3:5 clearly asserts, "Trust in the LORD with all your heart and lean not on your own understanding. (NIV)" I know that when the Apostle Paul wrote to his protégé, Timothy, in II Timothy 2:15, "Do your best to present yourself to God as one approved, a worker who does not need to be ashamed and who correctly handles the word of truth. (New Living Translation)" Paul was saying that to teach, preach, and to help others apply God's Word in their lives, we must ALL study and delve to the farthest depths of our understanding of the Word.

What must all successful workmen, no matter their trade, have and keep in perfect working condition? TOOLS! Too many Christians feel that if they have the King James Version (KJV) of the Bible, they are as in the vernacular of the streets, "good to go," as it relates to their Bible Studies! That is unfortunately a false premise, a somewhat naïve way of looking at studying God's Word. Those Christians who think the KJV is all they need to study the Word of God and that all other translations, such as The New International Version (NIV), The New Living Translation (NLT), or the Revised Standard Version (RSV) are not the true Word of God, do not realize that, unless they have and are using the "Authorized King James Version (AKJV)" of the Bible, they possess a translation of the original version of the King James Version published in 1611 AD.

So what I am saying? In addition to the KJV, a serious student of the Bible should at the very least possess a good Study Bible, a Strong's Exhaustive Concordance (so they might look up the Hebrew, Aramaic, and Greek word meanings in the Bible), a good Bible Dictionary (I suggest either The Nelson's or Wycliffe Bible Dictionary), and a good Bible Commentary (this tool helps explains the historical, grammatical and contextual meanings of the Scriptures). So, I strongly suggest that any true Bible student who wants to show themselves approved will have these tools in their Biblical Studies TOOLBOX!

Now with that being said, we must understand and apply the adage, "practice makes perfect." Truthfully, I do not believe that practice makes perfect. If we look at the world of professional sports, there are teams with athletes making multi-million dollar salaries that end each season with losing records, yet these teams practice as much or more than the Champions in that given sport! However, I do believe that the continued practice of Biblical Study does make our goal of achieving studious perfection more attainable! So, we must come to understand that there are 3 variations of approaches to in-depth analysis and study, no matter the discipline (Biblical, Scientific, Medical, Historical etc.). Just as in underwater exploration, the deeper the dive in our studies the greater the reward in terms of our acquired knowledge, in the learning process. This acquired knowledge will correspondingly lead to a greater degree of clarity of what we have learned.

I would like to compare these three approaches of studying the Word of God to my aforementioned analogy of underwater exploration compared to our in-depth study of God's Word. The first approach of underwater exploration is snorkeling. Snorkeling's greatest appeal is that it does not require the snorkelers to have a great deal of experience, requires minimal equipment and physical and intellectual effort, and provides the snorkelers with a sense of security as they usually stay near the water's surface in the event they encounter any difficulty. Snorkelers tend to stay near the shore in shallow water, thereby precluding their expansive view of the beauty of sea life and rock formations in that body of water. The second approach to underwater exploration is scuba diving. Unlike snorkeling, scuba diving requires more equipment in the form of an air tank and scuba diving suit for extended periods of being under water. Scuba diving gives the scuba divers more flexibility to explore the depths of the body of water they are in and allows them to see more of the sea bottom, and plant life of the body of water they are in. The greater the depth explored the greater the knowledge of what exists below the surface. The third and final approach to underwater exploration is deep sea diving. Deep sea diving requires not only a great deal of experience, but also certified training, more sophisticated equipment, and more time to be lowered to the deepest depths of water. There also is a connection to the deep sea diver to someone on a water craft for his/her air supply as they are lowered farther and farther into the depths of the sea. This connection allows them to see more for an extended period of time at or near the bottom of the water source. Deep sea divers, unlike snorkelers and scuba divers, see more of God's creations below the water's surface. Therefore, they have a greater appreciation of His/God's glory and power, but they are also dependent on others to reach distant depths below the water's surface.

So I ask, when you study God's Word, are you a snorkeler, a scuba diver, or a deep sea diver? Here is how you will know. If you only attend church, are totally reliant on the pastor's sermon, and read your Bible now and then without any of the tools I previously mentioned, you are a snorkeler. However, if you study the Word of God on a regular basis using the tools I mentioned, attend church, Bible Study, and / or Sunday School regularly, then you are a scuba diver. However, if, and this is a BIG IF, if you study the Word of God regularly on your own or with others using the tools I mentioned, attend church, Bible Study, and / or Sunday School regularly, and attend some Bible Teaching institution in your community, then you are a deep sea diver.

Given all that God has, is doing, and will do in our lives, how deep into His Word should we delve? Are our Biblical studies commensurate or equal to what God does for us, or do we give more time to frivolous activities, such as watching mind numbing reality TV shows? Do we spend an equitable amount of time studying the Word of God as we do with other things, such as trying to impress others with our material possessions, as opposed to trying to impress them with how our studies help us apply God's Word in our daily lives? Are we only fooling ourselves when we spend less than 10 minutes a day, if that, studying God's Word to show ourselves approved ... just something to think about, as we will not know when we are called home. We need to spend more time studying to show ourselves approved so we will only hear good things when our page in the Book of Life is opened in Heaven! I love what Dr. Benjamin Mays, President Emeritus of Morehouse University and mentor to Dr. Martin

Luther King once stated, "I would rather be prepared and have an opportunity and miss it, than to have an opportunity and not be prepared." Will we be prepared to answer God's opportunity to share His Word with others, or will we miss a glorious opportunity to serve Him because we were not prepared? I will leave you with an African Proverb, "not to know is bad, not to wish to know is worse!"

ARTICLE 5

Do You Have an Awe Inspiring Testimony?

Looking for Lena Horne: How The Lord Comforted Me While I was Temporarily Blind.

The story of Jesus' healing the blind man, located at John 9:25, is apropos for what I have endured of late. The King James Version (KJV) of God's word reads, "[25] He [the blind man] answered and said, whether he [Jesus] be a sinner or no, I know not: one thing I know, that, whereas I was blind, now I see."

During the period from May 5, 2014, through January 19, 2015 (Dr. Martin Luther King's Birthday Observance Day), I have had no less than four major eye surgeries on my right eye, my strongest eye!

As I endured these surgeries and their attendant recovery processes, the Lord kept, healed, and comforted me. Certainly, at this juncture, someone such as Bill Maher of the "Realtime With Bill Maher" Show on HBO might suggest that I am a fool for attributing the success of my surgeries to God. I must admit that I do like Bill Maher's Show but disagree with his anti-religious stance. Bill Maher is an intelligent man, one who is an avowed non-believer in God. He, or a believer of minimal faith, or even a nonbeliever might ask, "'what about the role of the surgeons and nurses involved in your operations? Why do you not give them credit for admirably performing their designated medical procedures?" To these individuals I would respond, "It was the Lord, not I who selected the very best glaucoma and detached retina surgeons and their entire staffs to attend to me. It was definitely the Lord who put me in the extremely capable hands of all the medical professionals who examined me and consulted one with the other about the complex issues of my case! It was only the Lord, who ensured that all the staff members of both my eye surgeons were always so professional, genuinely committed to their jobs, and truly a joy to encounter each and every time I had an appointment. It was the Lord who insured that the right people were on duty the days the surgical rooms were thoroughly cleaned, the surgical instruments were meticulously sterilized, the proper dosage of anesthesia was administered, and those who were involved in the registration and all the preliminary and post-surgical processes were performed with due diligence each and every time I entered the premise of where my surgeries were so thoroughly and miraculously performed! God had placed all the right people at the right place and at the right time to ensure the success of my eye surgeries!

I sincerely thank God for being the Chief surgeon, orchestrator, and the ultimate guide of the hands of everyone who touched me before, during, and after my eye surgeries.

But Brother James, how does this part of your story about having eye surgeries relate to your subtitle of this writing, *Looking for Lena Horne*?

I am ever so happy you asked me that question! You see, I have a four foot by sixteen inch collage of notable African American entertainers, writers, and civil rights leaders from the 1920s through the 1960s adorning a wall that leads from my kitchen to my family room in my home. Each of the photographs is black and white and is four by six inches in terms of their dimensions. In the frame closest to the family room the photograph of Lena Horne appears top row center.

After my surgery in September of 2014 my vision was diminished to the point where I was legally blind. As my sight slowly came back, I would look at the collage, but it was the photograph of Lena Horne that seemed to stand out like a lighthouse during a fierce storm on a very dark night. I looked at that photograph each day as I had the habit of eating in the family room in front of the big screen television. After each subsequent eye surgery, I would always look for the photograph each morning and all through the day as I entered my family room. I came to understand that the Lord was using this four by six inch photograph of Lena Horne to let me know that all would be fine; everything related to my sight would be better than ever.

It has often been said that God uses ordinary people to accomplish extraordinary things! Well, in my case, God clearly showed me that He will use something as simple as a black and white photograph of Lena Horne to let me know He loves me, and, as the word says, is with me always.

I get great comfort each and every day as my sight improves. I see the Lord's power of my prayers that my sight would be restored to its optimum level. My faith in God never wavered and has increased as the improvement in my sight is reaching fruition. So, that is why when I awake each day, I thank God for all He has done in my life, is doing in my life and will do in my life before I go downstairs looking for Lena Horne.

ARTICLE 6

What Would You Do If You Were Jesus For A Day?

I have a clear and distinct recollection of the old television prize game show, "Queen For A Day." Jack Bailey was the host, and three women would be selected from the studio audience to compete for prizes based upon which contestant, by virtue of applause, had the most convincing story of hardship and need.

The three contestants would share their hard-luck stories about their sick children or spouses, or the need for something as basic as a new refrigerator or washing machine. After being chosen by the studio audience's applause, Jack Bailey would crown the winner, "Queen for a Day."

I mention this because all of us are in need of something to spiritually, emotionally, intellectually, romantically, financially or otherwise enhance our personal circumstances.

Considering the power of Jesus and the Holy Spirit in our lives, what would you do if you were crowned, "Jesus for A Day"?

Would you wipe out worldwide poverty, eliminate all forms of disease, illness, racism, and sexism, and bring an abrupt end to violence and wars worldwide? Would you eradicate hunger all over the earth? Or, and this is a very BIG OR, would you be selfish and avenge past wrongs heaped upon you by others by destroying your enemies with catastrophes of Biblical proportion? Would you become richer than Warren Buffett and Bill Gates combined? Would you live the lifestyle of the rich and famous and have everyone, everywhere become a devoted celebriphile (a person who has an inordinate desire to always be socially intimate, romantically and / or sexually involved with a celebrity) and have these celebrities worship you as if you were deserving of the level of worship we should give to God?

Well, admittedly, I might not do the Biblically correct things that require immediate action to heal the socio-economic, aberrant politically-inspired, and environmental challenges such as ending global warming. I may not reeducate people with a distorted political slant and corrupt mentality. However, my focus would be on those who use their God-given gifts to enrich their lives in pursuit of what the Bible calls filthy "lucre"/money. So, this is what Brother James would do if I were crowned, "Jesus for a Day!" Yes, I would bring to an end all the ills that affect us, but I would identify with the masses all those who are nothing more than satanic gangsters and pimps in the pulpit. Here is what, (God, please forgive me) I would do if I were coronated "Jesus For a Day":

First, I would identify these vermin and scum masquerading as true men and women of God. I would:

- Impose a national salary cap on all ministers with having the cap commensurate to the cost of living in the locale that they preach. For example, given the cost of living in New York City, a pastor there would receive more salary than a pastor in Topeka, Kansas or Memphis.
- I would require all pastors on a quarterly basis to submit to a Maury Povich or Steve Wilkos type lie detector test where they would be required to answer questions such

as:
- Are you truly preaching the Word of God because that is your God-given calling, or are you preaching to become a well-known celebrity?
- Are you faithful to the Word of God, or are you using God's dynamic and blessed Word to become a millionaire?
- Are you faithful to your spouse, or do you engage in illicit extramarital affairs?
- Are you an abuser of alcohol or illegal drugs?
- Are you a pedophile?
- Do you use the services of a prostitute (male or female?)
- Do you rail from the pulpit about the evils of being a Gay, Lesbian, Bi-sexual or Transgender person while at the same time fit into one, if not ALL, of these alternative lifestyle categories yourself?
- Are you such a hypocrite that you smile on the faces of your congregants then go home and castigate and denigrate their Christian character in front of your family?
- Do you live in close proximity to your congregants by choice?
- Do you desire to serve God by being a servant and not an arrogant, condescending, pretentious overlord over the flock the Lord has entrusted to you to lead in their spiritual growth?
- Are you a dedicated student and correspondingly a teacher of God's Word?

Personally, I would not be surprised by the number of men and women of the cloth who would fail this test miserably! I can hear the lie detector test administrator while reading the results say something like, "and that was a Lie!" Or, "on the matter of... the lie detector test determined that you did not tell the Truth!"

Those who failed the polygraph test would be subject to the following punishment. They would have to:

- Wear a combination tether and taser like ankle device that would administer the maximum wattage/voltage allowed by law of a police taser each time they lied on their polygraph test and each time they committed an offense to God and His people.
- Work in a municipal improvement initiative as if they were members of a 1930s chain gang, keeping the streets and interstates free of trash. If you are too young to know what a chain gang was, Wikipedia.com provides us with an apt definition where it defines a chain gang thusly, "A **chain gang** is a group of prisoners chained together to perform menial or physically challenging work as a form of punishment. Such punishment might include repairing buildings, building roads, or clearing land. This system existed primarily in the southern parts of the United States, ... [until the mid 1950s.]"
- Work in a soup kitchen for two months a year on a rotational basis so they would not miss their turn on the chain gang.
- Visit the jails and prisons of their given community, teaching the inmates the true word of God. Please remember if they lie the taser would be activated!
- Study the Word of God 4 hours per day and be required to take a monthly Biblical knowledge test with a passing score of 95% or better. Should they fail the specific test, they would have to study 6 hours a day until they passed the test with a perfect score.
- Limit the spending on their automobile to $30,000 or less, and they could not purchase a new automobile for three years.

I would make any religious leader of a Christian faith suffer dire emotional, financial, and physical consequences for betraying God by misleading His people with the false gospels of planting a monetary seed to gain favor with God. I would punish all these pastors who teach tithing as opposed to giving, given the fact that there are two annual tithes of 20% annually and an additional (third) tithe due every three years. I would create hardship for those who steal from God, who take monies donated to a church by naïve congregants that wind up in the bank account of some greedy, narcissistic pastor.

So, should you find my punishment of those pastors, elders, bishops, and apostles etc. who use and abuse the word of God to enrich themselves extreme and harsh, you might want to look at what God has in store for them! II Peter 2 is explicit as to the punishment for these false teachers and pimps in the pulpit. The NIV translation of the Bible relates to us in II Peter 2:1-3, the following punishment:

False Teachers and Their Destruction

1 But there were also false prophets among the people, just as there will be false teachers among you. They will secretly introduce destructive heresies, even denying the sovereign Lord who bought them—bringing swift destruction on themselves. **²** Many will follow their depraved conduct and will bring the way of truth into disrepute. **³** In their <u>greed</u> these teachers <u>will exploit you</u> with fabricated stories. Their condemnation has long been hanging over them, and their destruction has not been sleeping.

Some might think my punishment of ungodly pastors

to be extremely harsh if I were to be crowned, "Jesus For A Day." However, when one considers II Peter in its entirety, my punishment pales in comparison to that which Almighty God would impose on these folks who have made themselves little "g" gods in the eyes of God's people!

Am I implying that all religious leaders are worthy of punishment? Absolutely not, as there are many pastors such as Pastor Jake Gaines, of the Synagogue Baptist Church of Detroit; Pastor Joseph Chatten, Pastor of Resurrection Mission Baptist Church, Berkley, Michigan; Pastor Levert Shell of Christian Faith Baptist Church, Detroit, and Pastor Linda Lunsford, Pastor of Faith Allegiance Full Gospel Baptist Church, New Albany, Indiana. Certainly these are not the only good pastors I know, but each in their own unique way are icons as to what my late father, Reverend Robert Walter James, alluded to when he said, "Jesus was the model preacher." I inferred from this comment that every pastor should aspire to be like Jesus in all they do. I am not saying that pastors should take a vow of poverty and live on the kindness of friends; however, pastors should preach the gospel of Jesus Christ and not the gospel of prosperity!

The aforementioned pastors all are dedicated workers in God's vineyard because they truly love God and not money. They all do what Jesus would do in every aspect of their lives.

Those who know me realize I have a major problem with and extraordinary levels of disdain for pimps in the pulpit.

Many churches are no more than cults of personality where the congregants attend their church because their pastor is charismatic, extremely articulate, and eloquent, even though they do not teach the true word of God. Richard

Pryor said on this subject as it relates to the African American Church, "N-Words love church because they get a show for their money!" I related in another book that there is a joke where a nonbeliever asked a believer what topic his pastor preached on Sunday, and the congregant enthusiastically responded, "I can't remember, but he sure did preach." By the way, what was the message and related scripture your pastor spoke on last Sunday?

You see, I have absolutely no respect for any pastor who uses the word of God as a means of making a living! Paul said that preachers should be compensated for preaching but did he mean they should be paid beyond their required subsistence level? If you said yes, what are the scriptures to support your position?

My father drove 132 miles one way before the completion of the interstate highway system in Kentucky to attend to his flock in a rural area in western Kentucky. He was paid a whopping $200 a month, most of which he used to maintain his vehicles and feed his family while in transport. The congregation also compensated my father with smoked meats, fresh eggs, and milk. That is the paradigm I operate from when I think about these preachers who own their own jet airplanes, live in the wealthiest neighborhoods, and have skyrocketing levels of personal income.

No, I am not hating on these pastors of wealth; I am questioning their true rationale for preaching the Word of God.

Well, I have shared what I would do if I were crowned "Jesus For A Day." Again, I ask respectfully, what would you do if you were "Jesus for a Day"?

ARTICLE 7

Is God Always Fair, and Does He Have to Be?

Okay, let us be very truthful! There are times in our lives when we might want to question Almighty God about His fairness. For instance, have you heard someone say something like this, "with all these bad people around committing all these heinous and incomparable acts, why did God take (please insert the name of someone you loved and admired who in your estimation died too soon here)? Why did God let (please insert the previously mentioned name of a loved one here) die so early. Why did God let one of His most devoted servants leave here suffering inordinate levels of physical pain? Truthfully, have YOU ever asked the following question? Why me Lord? Why me?

My beloved Mother, Juanita Mae Alexander James, passed on January 2, 2012. She was an excellent Sunday School Teacher, Cub Scout Den Mother, mentor to people young and mature alike. She served meals at the local Community Center, Oak and Acorns, to the centenarians, and she was known throughout the community as a gifted Christian missionary who went into bars, unsafe and unsavory neighborhoods to bring people into the Body of Christ. Should you not believe me, just ask the pastor and members of the Hill Street Missionary Baptist Church in Louisville, Kentucky. After she passed, I was told countless times by a myriad of people, "Your mom was my very best FRIEND!"

Brother James

There is one young lady in particular whom I will never forget who shared with me how my mother helped her through a very difficult period in her life. This beautiful and intelligent lady shared with me after my mother passed that she was hanging with the wrong crowd. Her life had digressed to its nadir, the absolute lowest point of her existence. She had become drug dependent to the extreme! She went on to say that her own family did not trust her and did not allow her into their homes. But, Miss James, as my mother was so fondly known, would allow her into her house and minister to her using God's Word. She related to me how she cried on my mother's shoulder and asked how she could get off drugs and turn her life around. My Mother's advice was succinct, bluntly to the point, and uniquely simple. She said my mom simply said, "What you might consider is a change of venue! Go somewhere where all your negative influences could be replaced with positive ones!" The young lady took my mother's advice, moved in with relatives in a small rural community where illicit drugs were not readily available, and through the Grace of God, become sober. This young lady returned to Louisville, became a college graduate, and is now recognized in the Midwest as a gifted and talented poet. Forgive me, but after hearing this and many similar testimonies about my mother, I was puzzled as to why the Lord allowed her to endure extreme pain in the last months of her life. I wondered what was the lesson for my family as we witnessed our beloved mother, sister, auntie, friend etc. die the way she did as opposed to dying quietly in her sleep. As a family, we watched our beloved loved one literally starve to death! Yes, I thought about what I perceived to be the Lord's unfairness as I know of many evil people who seem on the surface to be extraordinarily blessed with excellent health and an abundance of fine material blessings. Yes, I have made a list, a very long list of evil, pretentious, self-centered people who never go to church unless it is for a wedding or funerals and who are never heard to say anything positive about God who seem to be blessed. When I hear a good Christian has passed in pain or too early, I think about my list and ask God, Why? Why do you treat those who clearly DO NOT demonstrate their love for you BETTER than those who DO? So yes, I have questioned the Lord's fairness doctrine and have asked myself if God is fair.

Another example where one might question God's fairness occurred on Christmas Eve, 2015. A very popular, well known and accomplished musician in Detroit was on his way to drop off Christmas gifts to his three daughters who, if my memory serves me correctly, were between the ages of 4 and 12. He stopped at a gas station and was carjacked. The thieves, after taking his automobile, shot and killed him, even after he offered no resistance. This young man was an accomplished musician who was extremely popular because he was a genuine Christin man, but to add insult to injury, he was studying to become a Preacher of the Gospel of Jesus Christ! His greatest dream was to become an exemplary leader in the Christian community of Detroit! Many people questioned God's fairness as to why a good father and family man, friend, and talented musician who aspired to be a preacher of the Gospel of Jesus Christ exited this life in such a cruel and senseless manner. Can you feel the pain of his family and friends who might ask "Is God fair?"

"3" is God's number in the Bible for completion and perfection. Therefore, I have one last example to share with you regarding God's fairness. About 15 years ago, I met a woman who truly exemplified all the attributes of a virtuous, Christian woman. I met her through her cousin, Madeira Long, who was my Budget Analyst while I worked as an Information Technology Leader for the Internal Revenue Service.

Madeira's cousin and I met at a retirement party, and my first observation was that she was an intelligent woman of tremendous spirituality and great character. She was also very pleasing to the eye! I will never forget the outfit she wore when we met as it was very stylish and appropriate for the event we were attending. The sister knew how to dress! A few years later Madeira asked if her cousin could accompany her and her husband to an annual fish fry I host. Of course I said, "YES!" Madeira's cousin came for about ten years in a row and was not someone who went unnoticed. She was obviously spiritual, kind, and seemed to never meet a stranger. She would greet many of my guests and introduce herself. On Wednesday, March 8, 2016, I received a call from Madeira informing me that her beautiful, virtuous, spiritual cousin had passed away after going on a cruise and subsequently developing some digestive track problems. When Madeira told me of her cousin's passing, all I could say, rather Shout, was, "NO!" I subsequently attended the Home Going Service of my friend and was truly moved by all the sincere praise and accolades brought forth by those in attendance. The service was so uplifting that I left the sanctuary more enlightened and uplifted than saddened. Here was a woman that gave all to the Lord, her family, and her late husband of 43 years. I again pondered, is God fair and why did he take such a dedicated worker away from so many people who loved and needed her! I am truly blessed to have had Deborah Lorraine Mitchell in my life! I consider her a blessing in my life as my friend! I truly wish the Lord would have allowed you to meet her, but obviously that was not in His Divine plan. So, again, I asked myself, is God fair and why, given all the evildoers in the world, why did He take my friend, Deborah Lorraine Mitchell, home?

Have you posed the question why God allowed someone to get a job you richly deserved? Have you wondered why the monthly bills keep piling up in a monumental extreme in your house while you live within your means? Do you often wonder while you have regular church attendance and are a generous financial contributor to your house of worship that you still have to struggle each month to financially address your needs and not your wants? I am talking about your basic needs while your non-church going neighbors appear to be living well, extremely well. Please be real! Does it irritate you to the infinite degree that although you attend church regularly and are involved in a ministry, God seems to bless those who only make an appearance in church on Easter, Mother's Day, a funeral, or wedding? Do you sometimes feel that you are being PERSECUTED and God is ignoring you and your devotion to Him?

Well, join the club! I have been in your shoes! I, too have wondered why, and with all the devout Christian people I know who have made their transition to a holy place too soon or went out of this life in great pain, what God's message was for me! I can think of a multitude of people who should have preceded them in terms of leaving this earth. Please remember, I made a list of my candidates for an early exit from this planet due to their horrendous conduct.

Many of us have been taught that we should never, ever, I mean never, ever question God! But I have learned through scripture that God allows us to question His acts that we might perceive to be unfair as long as we pose these questions in a reverential and sincere manner. My proof is found in the Old Testament writings of the prophets Jeremiah and Habakkuk.

These prophets were contemporaries and raised complaints about God's fairness.

Jeremiah, chapter 12 is known as Jeremiah's

COMPLAINT. Let us look at a portion of this text so I may prove my point. The NIV translation of Jeremiah 12 reads thusly, "¹You are always righteous, LORD, when I bring a case before you. Yet I would speak with you about your justice: Why does the way of the wicked prosper? Why do all the faithless live at ease? ²You have planted them, and they have taken root; they grow and bear fruit. You are always on their lips but far from their hearts. *³Yet you know me, LORD; you see me and test my thoughts about you*. Drag them off like sheep to be butchered! Set them apart for the day of slaughter! ⁴How long will the land lie parched and the grass in every field be withered? Because those who live in it are wicked, the animals and birds have perished. Moreover, the people are saying, "He will not see what happens to us."

God answered Jeremiah later in chapter 12 when He stated, ⁵ "If you have raced with men on foot and they have worn you out, how can you compete with horses? If you stumble in safe country, how will you manage in the thickets by the Jordan? ⁶Your relatives, members of your own family—even they have betrayed you; they have raised a loud cry against you. Do not trust them, though they speak well of you.

⁷ "I will forsake my house, abandon my inheritance; I will give the one I love into the hands of her enemies. ⁸My inheritance has become to me like a lion in the forest. She roars at me; therefore I hate her. ⁹Has not my inheritance become to me like a speckled bird of prey that other birds of prey surround and attack? Go and gather all the wild beasts; bring them to devour. ¹⁰ <u>Many shepherds will ruin my vineyard and trample down my field;</u> they will turn my pleasant field into a desolate wasteland. ¹¹It will be made a wasteland, parched and desolate before me; the whole land will be laid waste because there is no one who cares. ¹² Over all the barren heights in the

desert destroyers will swarm, for the sword of the LORD will devour from one end of the land to the other; no one will be safe. ¹³ They will sow wheat but reap thorns; they will wear themselves out but gain nothing. They will bear the shame of their harvest because of the LORD's fierce anger."

¹⁴ This is what the LORD says: "As for all my wicked neighbors who seize the inheritance I gave my people Israel, I will uproot them from their lands and I will uproot the people of Judah from among them. ¹⁵ But after I uproot them, I will again have compassion and will bring each of them back to their own inheritance and their own country. ¹⁶ And if they learn well the ways of my people and swear by my name, saying, 'As surely as the LORD lives'—even as they once taught my people to swear by Baal—then they will be established among my people. ¹⁷ But if any nation does not listen, I will completely uproot and destroy it," declares the LORD.

If we were to review and critically analyze Habakkuk's Complaints in chapters 1 and 2, we would easily see the same questions being posed to God by this minor prophet. What is interesting is that Jeremiah and Habakkuk were contemporaries, one prophesying to the northern kingdom of Israel, and the other to the southern kingdom. Jeremiah was a major prophet and Habakkuk was a minor prophet to the divided nation of Israel, yet both had the same complaint posed to Almighty God! Simply put, their complaint was, is God FAIR? Habakkuk1:2-4 reinforces my point as the NIV asks,

² How long, LORD, must I call for help, but you do not listen? Or cry out to you, "Violence!" but you do not save? ³ Why do you make me look at injustice? Why do you tolerate wrongdoing? Destruction and violence are before me; there is strife, and conflict abounds. ⁴ Therefore the law is paralyzed, and justice never prevails. The wicked hem in the righteous, so that justice is perverted.

Can you see the similarity in these complaints of two of God's most devout servants? So, please know that it is reasonable to ask God questions as long as we do it respectfully and reverentially. I implore you to read Jeremiah 12 and Habakkuk 1 and 2 in their entirety so you may come to an understanding that God does things in mysterious ways His wonders to perform. Sometimes we fail to see the miracles we deem as tragic in our lives so God might accomplish something wonderful for all believers.

I am reminded of the adage: "Beauty is in the eyes of the beholder!" Well, in a similar vein, fairness stems from the perspective and vantage point of those who are the beneficiaries of fairness or those who feel they have been deprived of fairness in a particular situation.

Many years ago while I was an IT Leader at the IRS, a vacancy was announced for a promotional opportunity for a Branch Secretary. There were two applicants. One applicant was about 50 years old and had been rated as a Met or what one might consider academically a C+ performer throughout her career as a secretary. The other candidate was a 30 something woman of vastly less tenure at the IRS who had gone to Community College, took on additional assignments without being asked, and was more professional in the performance of her assigned duties. She was rated Distinguished or a B+ performer by all her supervisors. Given my exposure to both these ladies, I accepted the recommendation of my subordinate managers and selected the 30 something young lady for the position. When the other applicant learned she was not selected, she stormed into my office and threatened me with a Union Grievance. I told her she was well within her right to file a grievance, but she had just demonstrated why she was not selected by storming into my office without Union representation or an appointment.

Again, she was a C+ performer and did just enough work to get by. She never went out of her way to improve herself for any promotional opportunities as it related to her job and other possible job openings. She did absolutely nothing to improve her C+ rating/evaluation. She retorted that she should have gotten the position solely on the basis that she had more seniority than the other applicant. I bring this matter to your attention to make my point. The young lady who was promoted felt it fair that she was given the job because she had demonstrated her ability to perform at the next higher level and coupled her work ethic with her academic achievements. The other lady felt that she should have been promoted by virtue of the fact she had worked in the organization longer. She obviously felt that, in the words of Dr. Martin Luther King, "longevity has its merit" and longevity should trump better skill sets and education. She thought she had been treated unfairly. She subsequently filed a grievance against me and lost because when the applications of both candidates coupled with their performance in the interview process were considered, the recipient of the job stood head and shoulders over Ms. *BUT I HAVE BEEN HERE LONGER.*

I ask you, were my actions fair in terms of who should have been promoted? Please reflect on that question for just a moment. Okay, you have had enough time to deliberate on my question. You are absolutely correct, my actions WERE correct, just, and FAIR, no matter what either applicant thought!

Yes. I questioned God about the physical and emotional debilitating manner of the passing of my beloved mother. Yes, I questioned God about many situations I have seen and deemed unfair and viewed as an injustice to people who earnestly worked conscientiously for and loved the Lord.

Need I remind you of the Christmas Eve senseless murder of the young aspiring preacher or the unexpected passing of my virtuous, hardworking friend in God's metropolitan Detroit vineyard, Deborah Lorraine Mitchell?

Well, as I indicated earlier, fairness is a matter of one's perspective, depending on whether or not they see themselves on the winning or losing side in a given situation! But, let each of us be real and therefore FAIR!

When I think of what God has done, is doing, and will do in my life and the lives of my loved ones, we are truly BLESSED! More importantly, when I think about what God had His Son, Jesus, do for me, I have to keep every hardship, every defeat, every adverse situation I have faced in my life in its proper perspective! Clearly, what I have endured in my life is nothing compared to what Jesus endured for me and you and countless others!

I am at this writing, 67-year old. Jesus, the son of God only lived to be 33 years of age! I have evolved from abject poverty to a middle class existence while Jesus lived well below the poverty level for His day. Sure, I have been disappointed by many so-called friends, but I have yet to have any so-called friend turn me over to the authorities so I could be unfairly tried and sentenced to death due to the false accusations of others who I tried to help! No, I have never been imprisoned, then whipped mercilessly All Night Long, then humiliated by dragging a heavy wooden cross down a main street in Detroit while being cursed and spat upon by the masses. Nor have I suffered the egregious, humiliating indignities and scorn of those who would torment me and pierce my side with a spear while they put me to death in one of the world's most excruciating manners of capital punishment.

Yes, I have seen many situations go down in my life that I disagree with to this very day, but, I know my perceived hardships pale in comparison to the trials and tribulations Jesus faced in his adult life. In addition, I have a son, and I would not want to see him subjected to the treatment Jesus had in order to save humanity. No offense!

So, I politely and respectfully ask that the next time you think God is unfair, please think about Job or about the complaints of God's servants and prophets, Jeremiah and Habakkuk. Then ask yourself if your situation is worse than that of Jesus?

Know that God loves you, and as a Christian, I am commanded to love you too, even though we may never meet. Keep your head up looking to the Lord in difficult times, and please reflect upon the chorus lyrics of the Brooks and Dunn song "Believe," which state, "I raise my hands, bow my head I'm finding more and more truth in the words written in red They tell me that there's more to life than just what I can see I can't quote the book The chapter or the verse You can't tell me it all ends In a slow ride in a hearse You know I'm more and more convinced The longer that I live Yeah, this can't be No, this can't be No, this can't be all there is When I raise my hands, bow my head I'm finding more and more truth in the words written in red They tell me that there's more to life than just what I can see I believe Oh, II believe I believe I believe I believe I believe!!!"

My new bestest friends, I sincerely pray that you believe in the Lord because I do believe in the Lord with all my heart and soul! Yes, no matter what obstacles I face in my life, I BELIEVE!

ARTICLE 8

Are you a Punk Ass Christian?

Okay, my dear friends, before you start cursing me out about the title of this article, please allow me to define what I perceive to be a Punk Ass Christian!

The archaic and original definition of the word Punk is a "prostitute." The most common and contemporary use of the word Punk is "a worthless person." My definition of the word Punk is "a cowardly, wishy washy, no backbone individual who is afraid to take a stand on a principled issue for fear of being ostracized and criticized by the masses of their peers. In other words, they would rather go along with the flow of the crowd like sheep in order to be popular as opposed to having principles and integrity.

Some so-called Christians prostitute themselves to Satan by not taking a stand when they take the proverbial hear no evil, see no evil, speak no evil approach in the body of Christ. These Punk Ass Christians are part of a silent majority when things counter to God's Word are done. There are too many shameful and nefarious activities happening in the Houses of God, oftentimes orchestrated by the pastor. I would refer you to pimppreachers.com to validate my assertion.

I know of a church that operates a BYOB (Bring Your Own Bottle) cabaret hall, the church is trying to acquire a liquor license. Hmm, where does the spiritual nexus of a church owning and operating a cabaret hall fit into God's plan of salvation? I realize that I am only a quarter of an inch away from being qualified to be the village idiot, but the ownership and operation of a cabaret hall by any church do not resonate with me!

The protest of the congregation was nil because most are afraid to speak up and be in opposition to the pastor and his greedy wishes.

These same Punk Ass Christians have sat by idly while their egomaniacal, extremely low self-esteem pastor systematically eliminated the best singers and musicians, the most dedicated ministry heads, and the very best Sunday School Teachers. Why? Well, this pimp in the pulpit is lazy and even pulls many of his sermons directly from websites such as, sermonsonline.com on the internet. I believe that qualifies as plagiarism! His self-esteem from a psychological standpoint is at its nadir, its absolute lowest point! He is so vain and inept that anyone in the congregation who appears to have greater knowledge of God's Word is considered a threat. He is so afraid of losing his members that he has used the same three pastors at his last four Pastor's Anniversary's. Why? If any pastor gets more amens than this megalomaniac, he or she will NEVER be invited back to preach. This is a travesty to God's people in the church I am alluding to, given the wealth of pastors in the metropolitan Detroit area! What confident man or woman of God launches into a diatribe about the lack of amen's, then hollers at the ushers and tells them to open the doors at the rear of the sanctuary so the non amen-ing congregants may leave and go hear a popular pastor in that community? Not hating on my brother, just speaking the TRUTH!

The Punk Ass Christians just sat in their seats sheepishly and whispered their discontent and endured this unwarranted tongue-lashing just out of earshot of this maniacal pimp in the pulpit. No one, not a Deacon, Trustee, Ministry Head or any congregants approached this man and expressed their dismay about the inappropriateness of his egregious comments directed to them! Punk Ass Christians, huh?

Now let us look at the archaic and contemporary definitions of an Ass so you might fully understand what I am implying rather strongly to be a Punk Ass Christian!

An Ass in Biblical times was a dumb animal relegated to endure life as a beast of burden. An Ass in contemporary terms is a person's behind that God designed for us to sit on, and this word is correspondingly used to define a foolish or stupid person.

Let us look at a Biblical example of a Punk Ass Christian found in the Parable of the Good Samaritan (Luke 10:25-37 NIV). [25] On one occasion an expert in the law stood up to test Jesus. "Teacher," he asked, "what must I do to inherit eternal life?" [26] "What is written in the Law?" he replied. "How do you read it?" [27] He answered, "'Love the Lord your God with all your heart and with all your soul and with all your strength and with all your mind'; and, 'Love your neighbor as yourself.' [28] "You have answered correctly," Jesus replied. "Do this and you will live." [29] But he wanted to justify himself, so he asked Jesus, "And who is my neighbor?" [30] In reply Jesus said: "A man was going down from Jerusalem to Jericho, when he was attacked by robbers. They stripped him of his clothes, beat him and went away, leaving him half dead. [31] A priest happened to be going down the same road, and when he saw the man, he passed by on the other side. [32] So too, a Levite, when he came to the place and saw him, passed by on the other side. [33] But a Samaritan, as he traveled, came where the man was; and when he saw him, he took pity on him. ³⁴ He went to him and bandaged his wounds, pouring on oil and wine. Then he put the man on his own donkey, brought him to an inn and took care of him. ³⁵ The next day he took out two denarii and gave them to the innkeeper. 'Look after him,' he said, 'and when I return, I will reimburse you for any extra expense you may have.'

³⁶ "Which of these three do you think was a neighbor to the man who fell into the hands of robbers?"

³⁷ The expert in the law replied, "The one who had mercy on him." Jesus told him, "Go and do likewise."

We see that the people in this parable who could have and should have helped the robbery victim did absolutely nothing to help him. They probably said to themselves, "Let the Lord help this man!"

Please understand that to the ancient Israelites, the Samaritans were considered a low-class and vastly inferior people. According to the Nelson's New Illustrated Bible Dictionary and the Smith's Bible Dictionary, the Samaritans were enemies of the ancient Israelites. The Samaritans were of Assyrian descent who intermarried with the idolatrous pagan people who co-existed in the territory encompassing ancient Israel and

Samaria. The ancient Israelites considered them "half breeds" and looked upon them with great contempt and disdain. Therefore, the Samaritans were an ignoble race of people; inimical to Jehovah in the eyes of many Old and New Testament era Jews. But it was the Samaritan who displayed the Christian love to the victim of the mugging, NOT the Punk Ass Priest or the Levite believers of Jehovah! These cowardly men opted to "Let the Lord help" this distressed man! Oh, I say and say again the refrain and chorus of a Punk Ass Christian in negative situations is, "Just let the Lord handle it!" And what amazes me about this story/parable, given the fact that the robbery victim was virtually naked, is how did the Priest and Levite not know if he was one of their countrymen, a neighbor, or a kinsman? What would you have done in a similar situation? Would you allow fear of being in a crime ridden area to prevent you from helping someone in distress? With the proliferation of cellphones, would you at least make a call to 911? At the very least the Levite should have offered some assistance as the Mosaic Law stipulated the Levites were sanctified to be the maintainers of all the affairs of the Tabernacle. One of their daily roles was the food distribution from the "Store House." The truth of tithing laws teaches us there were three tithes. Two that were a tenth of the herds and produce from the fields. These two tithes or ten percent were to be collected by the Levites annually. The first tithe was the "tithe unto the Lord (to be collected annually)." The second tithe was known as the "Feast of Festival/Feast of Tabernacle tithe (to be collected annually)." The third tithe was an additional tithe to support the widows, orphans and aliens distressed in the Israelites controlled lands (collected only every third year). Please do the math! Two tithes of ten percent annually give us a total annual tithing obligation of 20% the first and second year of the tithing period with an additional 10% due in the third year of the tithing period. This third tithe's purpose is found in Deuteronomy 26:12 (^{12}When you have finished setting aside a tenth of all your produce in the third year, the year of the tithe, you shall give it to the Levite, the foreigner, the fatherless and the widow, so that they may eat in your towns and be satisfied. NIV). So, what was the Levite supposed to do? Should he have gone to the town, gathered a few other men, then go back and tend to the robbery victim? Wasn't the robbery victim distressed in the lands controlled by the Israelites? But, no, the Levite simply let the Lord handle this dangerous situation where someone he was obligated to help was in need!

I pray that I will do the right thing where I could be a Good Samaritan in adverse circumstances where my assistance is required.

I know someone is pondering if I am being blasphemous because God is all-powerful, all-knowing, always present and in control. So, does God need our help to right the wrongs we witness in our lives and the lives of others? NO, absolutely not! He does not need our help in any ungodly circumstances where instances of injustice, inequality, or hatred etc. reign supreme. However, Jesus and the Apostles were all community activists. They spoke against the mistreatment of the poor and socially and politically disadvantaged of their day. They brought the leaders of the Pharisee Party to task as well as the rule of the dominant Roman Empire. Again, they were the community activists in the first century AD of the ancient world. The Word of God clearly asks us a poignant and relevant question in Genesis 4:9, "Am I my brother's keeper?" Are we our sisters and brothers keepers? Yes, we are! The Scriptures teach us that God has and will use PEOPLE to fight His battles. For example, God used the Egyptians and Babylonians to capture, enslave and disperse His disobedient Chosen people. God also used people in the New Testament era, and all one needs to do is refer to the works of the first century AD Jewish historian, Josephus, to validate my assertion. Josephus wrote in great detail about how God used the Roman Empire to destroy the city of Jerusalem for a second time in 70AD. This destruction was due to the constant infighting within the besieged walls of Jerusalem by two opposing disobedient groups of Jewish zealots. The Romans were on the outside of the walled city of Jerusalem, but the

Jews were fighting each other on the inside! This warfare led to the second dispersal of many ancient Jews from the Promised Land.

In a contemporary sense, God has used people, not floods, hurricanes, etc. to destroy those He considers to be His enemies or disobedient children. Just Google the scandals involving prominent pastors in this country. Does anyone remember Jim and Tammi Faye Bakker, Jimmy Swaggart, Jim Jones, Pastor Zachary Tims, Reverend Ted Haggard, Eddie Long, etc.? I do, and this is just a partial list of disobedient pastors brought down by brave Christians who simply spoke up!

A contemporary example the Lord provides of Punk Ass Christians was presented by Dr. Martin King in his profoundly eloquent and noteworthy, Letter From A Birmingham Jail. This letter written during Dr. King's eleven day incarceration for leading a peaceful civil disobedience protest, chastises the Euro-centric American clergy both in the north and south who suggested he was moving too fast in his attempt to bring about integration. Dr. King's peaceful thrust for integration was intended to bring an end to discrimination, segregation, and all forms of inequality not only in the USA but also worldwide. These Punk Ass Christians implored Dr. King as the leader of the Civil Rights Movement to: slow down, be patient, and let the Lord handle and resolve the issues surrounding inequality throughout this country. I can hear these Punk Ass Christian's telling their congregations to pray for the negatively impacted "Negro" people and their leaders to acquiesce to their second class citizenship because one day, oh Lord, one day love and equality would reign supreme throughout this land. However, these Punk Ass Christians were not being subjected and subjugated to abject poverty, underemployment, and inadequate and inferior education, so it was easy for them to suggest to Dr. King that he be inordinately patient.

Yes, these Punk Ass Christians preached a gospel to Dr. King that one day the Lord would handle the issue of inequality by touching the hearts, minds, and souls of the KKK, White Citizen's Council, and other white supremacist groups who "legally" disenfranchised and subjected people of color, especially African Americans, to a second class citizenship status!

These Punk Ass Christians obviously thought that their support of Dr. King would adversely impact their privileged status in their safe, discrimination and lynching-free communities. I am reminded of the words in a poem written by Martin Niemöller, a Protestant pastor and ardent critic of Adolph Hitler. To the best of my recollection, pastor Niemöller wrote, "When they first came for the Jews, I was not Jewish, so I said nothing and did nothing. Then one day they came for the socialist and communist, but I was neither of these, so I said nothing and did nothing. Then one day they came for the trade unionist, the sick and feeble, but I was none of these, so I said nothing, and I did nothing. Then one day they came for me and there was no one left to speak up for me!

Niemöller's point and the equally powerful rebuttal made in Dr. Kings Letter From A Birmingham Jail, clearly suggest we must not be afraid to stand up and speak out against injustice, tyranny, and inequality anyplace at anytime! Oh, I love the profound sentiment of Dr. King when he stated, "The ultimate measure of a man is not where he stands in moments of comfort and convenience, but where he stands at times of challenge and controversy."

I realize there are times where if we stand up for what

is right, we might not lose our lives but could lose our livelihood! But sometimes conditions warrant our taking a stand just as countless citizens from across this country did for decades to bring an end to segregation and its attendant ills. We do not have the courage of our Lord and Savior who endured the 40 lashes of the Roman scourging prior to His crucifixion to prove our love for and dedication to God. After all, Jesus made this sacrifice to grant us the privilege of Salvation. We then must never be heard saying something in the context of, "Let the Lord handle it." No, we must never be like the Priest and the Levite in the parable of the Good Samaritan where we see wrong done to others and do nothing! It is inconceivable to see any segment of this or any other society being deprived of their human rights and yet say nothing and do nothing!

     Yes, we must address the ills that adversely impact us and other folks in similar or dissimilar distress! Instead of saying, "I am going to let the Lord handle this," why not say, exuberantly, "Lord, I got this because I am empowered by You! Is that not what Jesus did? He could have exerted His influence with His Father God and lived like a king on earth. Instead, He chose to hang out and help those who suffered from social, economic, and political poverty! What would Jesus do and what must we do to go to heaven and be called when our chapter in the Book of Life is opened. Yes, we all will one day be held accountable for all we did and did not do to honor God in our lives. We all will be called out for all we said and did not say in terms of our Christian principles. Will we be equipped for the protracted battle against the forces of evil like the apostle Paul who wrote in Ephesians 6:10-18, [10] Finally, be strong in the Lord and in his mighty power. [11] Put on the full armor of God, so that you can take your stand against the devil's schemes. [12] For our struggle is not against flesh and blood, but against the rulers, against the authorities, against the powers of this dark world and against the spiritual forces of evil in the heavenly realms. [13] Therefore put on the full armor of God, so that when the day of evil comes, you may be able to stand your ground, and after you have done everything, to stand. [14] Stand firm then, with the belt of truth buckled around your waist, with the breastplate of righteousness in place, [15] and with your feet fitted with the readiness that comes from the gospel of peace. [16] In addition to all this, take up the shield of faith, with which you can extinguish all the flaming arrows of the evil one. [17] Take the helmet of salvation and the sword of the Spirit, which is the word of God.

So, on that glorious day when we stand before the bar of judgment, will our record suggest that we were stalwart warriors and emissaries for Jesus, or will our record clearly indicate we were Punk Ass Christians?

ARTICLE 9

Did God Call You To Sit On The Bench?

I am blessed to know many very gifted and talented people. Some of these folks are gifted artistically, while others are gifted intellectually, or athletically. Those that I know with ability on some sports teams all strived for a "starting" position on the team where their gift could best be utilized.

None of these gifted athletes to my knowledge went out for a specific team position just to sit on the bench, satisfied just to be seen in their bright colored team uniform.

Now with that context in mind, why does it appear that so many people who profess to be called to preach the Gospel of Jesus Christ seem so comfortable to sit in an elevated position in a pulpit controlled by someone whom God has called to be the under-shepherd of that given congregation? Certainly, those who are truly called should never assume that they are automatically qualified and called to preach without being guided and taught by a true shepherd of God's people. But, and this is a big but, why, after being ordained, would one sit in a pulpit week after week waiting for their turn to preach, especially when their turn is determined by someone who has the overall responsibility to lead the church to which God assigned them? When a minister is unable to frequently use his or her gifts of preaching the Lord's word, where is the benefit to God's people? The National Football League (NFL) usually has 55 players who dress for games, but do they all get a chance to get into the game each week?

One might assume that the minister waiting his or her turn to preach does so because they are content to be seen and recognized as the student of Pastor So-and-So, just as the disciples were students and under-studies of our Lord and Savior.

However, the day came when all the disciples were sent out on their own to teach and preach the gospel. Their title and role of a disciple and student was changed to that of an Apostle which means, "one sent forth"!

When we reflect upon God's word, could we, or should we assume that each of the disciples who later became Apostles had equal gifts? There were only four Gospels written, but there were twelve disciples. When we look at the epistles to the churches founded in the first century AD, only Paul, Peter, James, and John wrote letters/epistles that were deemed worthy of insertion in the King James Bible. My point, simply put, is that each of the disciples, except Judas, made major contributions to the building of the Christianity that exists to this very day. So, did the other disciples who became Apostles just sit idly by and let Peter, James, John, and Paul do all the teaching and preaching? Did these other Apostles just sit on the bench? No, they all went forth, and at the cost of being martyred, became preachers of the gospel. All one needs to do is consult a book, such as the Encyclopedia of Biblical Characters and/or Men and Women of the Bible, and one would easily see that the other disciples who did not contribute writings to the Bible all did their jobs of teaching and preaching the gospel with due diligence, as again they all lost their lives for carrying God's message throughout the then known world. They were not content to just sit on the bench or stand in the shadow of those whose words we read in the gospels, epistles, and other books of the New Testament.

Does the perception that a pastor of a given church has greater gifts than those ministers he has taught and ordained indicate that they are to stay under that pastor's tutelage forever? Or, should the day come as it did with Jesus in the 16th chapter of the Gospel of John where He told the disciples He was leaving them so they might carry out their assigned calling to preach the gospel? **Should a pastor not** tell and encourage his sons in the ministry to move on and start their own church?

I am reminded at this juncture of the details in I Corinthians 9:1-2 where Paul had to defend his God-given authority to be called an Apostle; one who would teach and preach to the Gentiles. What did Paul do? Did he acquiesce? Did he just politely go and sit in the corner of the room where the other Apostles had gathered without any form of protest? Did he go and sit on the bench at the town square? No, he stood his ground and proved beyond the shadow of a doubt that he was chosen by God to be the Apostle to the Gentiles.

Now, what about that young protégé of Paul's named Timothy who some refer to as a "Momma's boy?" He followed Paul's explicit instructions to preach and teach to the congregations in Ephesus, even though he would have to overcome the obstacles of a young man leading the elders and being a stranger to that given community of churches. And yes, since we are on a roll right about now, what about that guy named Titus, whom Paul also mentored in an epistle and sent to the island of Crete, where the indigenous population was known for their immorality, idolatry, and simply put, their uncouth behavior?

My point is if people have truly been called to preach

the gospel, why would they not start a church in their own home just like the churches in the first century AD were established?

If that is not an option, why would they not go to every church in their local community asking the pastors of the churches to give them a chance to preach? This would afford them to get some exposure? Unfortunately, however, too many ministers are content to simply be that, not a pastor or even an ordained minister, rather, they are content to happily sit in the pulpit on the bench. Yes, some folks would rather sit in the pulpit, on the bench of another man or woman of God. They would rather just be seen every Sunday for two hours in an elevated position where they do not assist the poor and down-trodden of their communities. Nor, do they lead a nursing home ministry, or, a jail ministry, or a feed-the-homeless ministry. Hey, why not seek the opportunity to preach at a homeless shelter? I truly believe if one is called, then God has a place for those he calls. We might find ourselves in situations like the Apostle Paul by constantly having to prove ourselves to others who think their teaching and preaching skill sets are much superior to ours. Or, perhaps we will find ourselves in a situation like Timothy and have to prove to others older than us we have a gift and anointing placed upon us by God to preach and teach, thereby, moving beyond their constant criticism. Moreover, we may have to gird our loins like Titus to teach and preach in an environment where those we are trying to bring into the kingdom of God are idol worshippers of the gods of money, status, power, fame, and fortune.

I am chronologically mature enough (this is my polite way of avoiding the use of the term old enough!) to remember the 1950s, TV show, "The Ernie Kovac Show." In one of his comedic routines, there were two football players sitting on the end of the team bench with their bench warmer coats on. As the skit progresses, several key players on the team were hit with severe injuries, such as broken limbs. The coach would look down the bench and see the two players who had yet to enter the game. Rather than send them into the game, he pleaded and cajoled the severely injured players to stay in the game so he would not have to make any substitutions. This went on for several minutes when a whistle blew indicating the two minute warning before the game's end. With two minutes left in the game the two bench-warmers arose and headed for the locker room. It was readily apparent that these players knew their services and skills would not be used in that or any other game because as they took off their bench warmer jackets, they had dressy, business clothes underneath. They commented about taking off their cleats and putting on their dress shoes, and then they headed for the nearest bar or nightclub to party.

I hope this illustration helps make my point that if you make it on God's team, strive to be an active player and not a bench warmer. There is a virtual plethora, a cornucopia of bench warmers in the numerous houses of God in this country. The interrogatory that now remains is, are you a star performer or simply content to ride the bench on God's team at your chosen house of worship? Why don't we scrutinize that question for a few minutes!

What would Jesus and the Apostles of the first century AD church do? Or better yet, what did they do? Hmm, if the word "Christian" means "Christlike" what should we do?

ARTICLE 10

Is it a Sin for Christians to Drink Alcohol?

Recently, I was invited to join a conversation at an outing where the following question was asked, "Should Christians drink alcohol?" The follow-up question was, "Is drinking alcohol a sin"?

There were two opposing camps on the issue. One group thought that drinking alcohol was a heinous sin. The other camp was in favor of consuming alcohol as long as it was consumed in moderation. I politely reminded both groups that the drinking of wine was mentioned many times throughout both the Old and New Testaments. According to the Strong's Exhaustive Concordance of the Bible, wine is mentioned 230 times in the Bible.

There are some Christians today who would love to see a reinstitution or return to the laws of the Prohibition era. Consulting Wikipedia.com, we found information about the Prohibition era in the United States.

Prohibition in the United States was a nationwide constitutional ban on the sale, production, importation, and transportation of alcoholic beverages that remained in place from 1920 to 1933. It was promoted by the "dry" crusaders, a movement led by rural <u>Protestants</u> and social Progressives in the Democratic and Republican parties, and it was coordinated by the Anti-Saloon League and the <u>Woman's Christian Temperance Union.</u> Prohibition was mandated under the Eighteenth Amendment to the U.S. Constitution. Enabling legislation, known as the Volstead Act, set down the rules for enforcing the ban and defined the types of alcoholic beverages that were prohibited. For example, <u>religious uses</u> of wine were allowed. Private ownership and consumption of alcohol was not made illegal under federal law; however, in many areas local laws were stricter, with some states banning possession outright. Nationwide Prohibition ended with the ratification of the Twenty-first Amendment, which repealed the Eighteenth Amendment, on December 5, 1933.

So, are there any scriptures in the Bible that would warrant a nationwide or an international ban on the sale and use of alcoholic beverages? Were there any scriptures that would prohibit all Christians from imbibing wine and other alcoholic drinks?

Well, I believe there are four major bans in the Bible about the consumption of alcohol; however, we must analyze them carefully so we may come to a complete, educated, and truthful understanding to the question, "should Christians drink alcohol?

The first prohibition on the use of alcohol is found in Leviticus 10:9, where the consumption of wine in the tent of meetings was expressly forbidden. That makes complete sense to me. Could you imagine a religious service where every congregant had the opportunity to drink alcohol throughout the service? Can you see the potential distractions? People would become less inhibited, and as we used to say in the streets, get loose! I can hear the people who have a drink or two say, "I'm feeling the spirit!" But is this the spirit that the Lord would want them to experience? I can hear the chants now, "Party over here!" Wait a minute! Do you hear another popular chant? "The roof, the roof, the roof is on fire. We don't need no water, Let the ... burn."

Of course I am being facetious, but I think I made my point that a prohibition of drinking alcohol in God's house should be easily understood, supported, and enforced.

The second prohibition against drinking alcohol is found in Numbers chapter 6 and deals with the vow of a Nazarite. The word Nazarite means "to consecrate" or "to be separated." A Nazarite was an individual (in ancient Jewish society a man, or a woman, but usually a man) who made a vow to consecrate himself or herself for God's purposes which could include a ministerial assignment for a specific period of time. This specified period of the vow could be months, years, or even his or her entire life. According to The Nelson's and Wycliffe Bible Dictionaries, there were three prohibitions for a Nazarite after they swore an oath or made a vow to consecrate themselves to God. One, a Nazarite was not to consume anything produced by a grapevine. This prohibition would include the non-consumption of grapes and any grape byproducts, such as grape seeds, wine, vinegar, and raisins. Two, A Nazarite was forbidden from cutting his hair during his period of separation and consecration. Samson was a Nazarite and we know what happened to him when he was duped by Delilah who cut his hair. Third, a Nazarite was to avoid at all cost any contact with a corpse, even if it was a family member. During this consecrated period a Nazarite was to keep himself ritually clean every day.

The third major Biblical prohibition concerning drinking alcohol is found in both the Old and New Testaments where there are warnings about being drunk, or should I say, intoxicated. The Old Testament prohibition about drunkenness is located at Isaiah 5:11. The New International Version of God's word reads thusly, "11 Woe to those who rise early in the morning to run after their drinks, who stay up late at night till they are inflamed with wine." Do you know anyone with whom you would love to share this Biblical admonishment? Do you know anyone who, as the O'Jays song goes is, "Living for the weekend" and living for the weekend is their time spent in the clubs?

The New Testament prohibition against being intoxicated is found in Ephesians 5:18. The NIV translation of God's word reads, "18 Do not get drunk on wine, which leads to debauchery. Instead, be filled with the Spirit." I just love how the word of God is validated from the Old Testament to the New. It appears at this juncture we can assume that drinking alcohol is neither Biblically banned nor a sin. The sin that accompanies consuming alcoholic beverages is drinking to the point of intoxication. I remember a saying from my childhood, "there are only two types of drunks, a happy drunk and a mean drunk, and both will regret their drinking the morning after!" It is the morning after that people who had too much to drink will pay homage to the porcelain goddess and promise God, they will never, ever drink like that again if only He, God, will give them some quick relief. I am honest, so I must admit that in my past, and I repeat, in my past, there were times I had been out to a club and woke up the next morning wondering how I made it home after a night of heavy drinking. I strive to be a paragon of truth, and I must admit when it comes to having drunk alcohol in excess, I have been there!

The fourth and final major Biblical prohibition against drinking alcohol concerns encouraging weaker Christians to drink. This prohibition about encouraging weaker Christians to sin is located at I Corinthians 8:9-13. The NIV translations for this scripture reads, "⁹Be careful, however, that the exercise of your rights does not become a stumbling block to the weak. ¹⁰ For if someone with a weak conscience sees you, with all your knowledge, eating in an idol's temple, won't that person be emboldened to eat what is sacrificed to idols? [11] So this weak brother or sister, for whom Christ died, is destroyed by your knowledge. [12] When you sin against them in this way and wound their weak conscience, you sin against Christ.[13] Therefore, if what I eat causes my brother or sister to fall into sin, I will never eat meat again, so that I will not cause them to fall." While this block of scripture does not address drinking alcohol specifically, there is a general and guiding principle that doing anything sinful in front of a believer whom you have influence over is inappropriate and may become an impediment to another's spiritual growth. If we were to replace all references to eating meat with drinking alcohol, then the essence and context of this scripture of our not influencing others to sin is one and the same. I have learned that if I know someone who has a drinking problem, I will make sure that when I am around them, I do not tempt them to drink by having alcohol in their presence. Some might say this is hypocritical of me, but I would say in response that my actions are geared to not cause another with a drinking problem to be adversely influenced by my actions. That is what the Apostle Paul is obviously addressing here. We must be sure not to influence others to sin! If you are in any public setting, know that someone is watching your every move. If you are known to be a Christian, know that someone is watching you and may report your actions to others saying you are a big hypocrite. Others will be watching you because they admire and respect you and want to emulate your every move. In either case, what we do can have its repercussions, and we should strive to do things that are pleasing in God's sight!

So, are we getting closer to a better understanding of what the word of God really says about drinking alcohol?

Many Christians adhere to whatever statute of the

Mosaic Law (there are 613 Mosaic laws) that supports their position on a particular Biblical issue, such as temperance, the non-consumption of alcohol. However, we are no longer under the law, but under the grace of Jesus Christ. The Apostle Paul informs us in Romans 6:14, For sin shall no longer be your master, because you are not under the law, but under grace (NIV).Therefore, since we are no longer under the law but under grace we will find in the New Testament that drunkenness is discouraged and considered a sin and encouraging others to drink in excess is also discouraged. A careful review of the word of God would readily show us wine and the drinking thereof were things that Jesus and the Disciples did apparently on a regular basis. Even the Apostle Paul condoned drinking wine because the purity of drinking water in the first century AD was obviously not as pure as it is today. Paul said in I Timothy 5:23, "Stop drinking only water, and use a little wine because of your stomach and your frequent illnesses" (NIV). Hmm, seems like Paul was advising his young protégé, Timothy, to keep a little wine around the house for "medicinal purposes"!

For further clarity, let us now look at what Jesus did and said, as related to the consumption of alcoholic beverages.

Regarding the drinking of alcohol you are probably thinking right now, what would Jesus do? Well, I pose the question, in terms of drinking wine, what did Jesus do?

The NIV Study Bible has a list of all the miracles Jesus performed. Jesus' first miracle recorded in John 2:1-11 was to turn water into wine, or as I heard a TV evangelist say, "Jesus turned H2O into Merlot. This miracle showing Jesus' power was manifested at a wedding party. The custom of the day was for the host of the wedding to serve expensive wine to his guest first, and when that ran out he would set out cheap wine hoping his guest drank so much of the former they would not notice an appreciable difference to the taste of the latter. However, after Jesus turned the water into wine, the host said it was even better than the one he had first set out for his guest. It seems to me if our Lord and Savior had reason to ban wine under any circumstance for Christian clean living, He would not have turned water into wine. His miracle could easily have been that He made the water so pure it healed all in attendance who were ill. Or, He could have made the water so potent that instead of a fermented grape juice high, the guest would have received a high from the Holy Water and the Holy Spirit. I think Jesus turned water into wine because He drank wine at such events.

I think it is of tantamount importance that we look at what Jesus said in Matthew 11:18-19 and Luke 7:33-34 about how He and John the Baptist were viewed by His detractors. In Matthew 11:18-19 Jesus said, "18 For John came neither eating nor drinking, and they say, 'He has a demon.' 19 The Son of Man came eating and drinking, and they say, 'Here is a glutton and a drunkard, a friend of tax collectors and sinners.' But wisdom is proved right by her deeds." The reference to "Son of Man" is a reference to Jesus. In the Old Testament this term was used to indicate Jesus and all mankind, while the term Spirit was an Old Testament reference to the Holy Spirit/Ghost.

Now, if what we just read is not a clear indication that Jesus drank wine, I have no idea what other statement could be more pointed or profound to lead us to the truth. Jesus drank wine, possibly on a regular basis! If we break down this scripture, Jesus said "The Son of Man came eating and drinking." This statement could easily be rewritten to say, "When I came both eating and drinking ..." I return to my original question, "What did Jesus do?" Well, it is readily apparent that Jesus was not one to imbibe just for the sake of it. Rather, Jesus drank wine as part of the social custom of His day. I remember being in French class in Junior High School and my instructor said he had toured Europe with the famed Fisk University Singers. He told us it was the custom in France for the entire family to have wine with their dinner because a lot of food was cooked with butter and the wine was an agent to cut down on what we now know to be high cholesterol. It is important that I mention it included any person at least twelve years old. That was the custom of the sixties and this practice may still occur to this day. In simple terms, drinking wine in the first century AD was probably the norm, and Jesus just fit in with everyone else. Remember, there were no water purification systems like we have today. Wine might have been used as a preventive poor health measure.

If we were to look closely at Jesus' words in Matthew 26:29, Jesus admits to drinking wine to His Disciples at the Last Supper. At the Last Supper, while Jesus was serving His Disciples and preparing them for what was about to happen to Him, Jesus Said, "29 I tell you, I will not drink from this fruit of the vine from now on until that day when I drink it new with you in my Father's kingdom." In essence, Jesus was telling His Disciples that He had His last drink of earthly wine with them and He would not have another drink until they were all reunited in heaven, where they would drink a heavenly wine. Again, I respectfully suggest to you that Jesus was not a drunkard as His critics suggested. Rather, He was a social drinker to help those around Him who were in awe of Him feel more comfortable in His Divine presence. If I may offer a contemporary analogy, what Jesus did by drinking wine was similar to President Barack Obama shooting hoops with folks at the White House. Everyone who has shot basketball with the President saw him in a different, and must I say relaxed light. He was just, "one of the guys."

I think one could easily postulate that there are no Biblical prohibitions concerning drinking alcoholic beverages. We now know that the sin directly related to drinking alcohol is that of drunkenness and encouraging others who have a propensity to drink alcohol to drink.

As a Christian, I admit to having a drink every now and then. I might have a drink with some friends while out to dinner. I might have a drink while watching a sporting event in the confines of my home. Or, I may even have a drink at a wedding reception, retirement party, or some other event.

I know the consequences of drinking and driving due to the proliferation of ads on television discouraging drunk driving. I also know that if we exercise good judgment, we can have a drink socially outside of our homes.

I leave you with this notion in the form of a question. What would Jesus do? I know from what I have read He would never get drunk but would love to have a good time in the presence of His family and friends. After all, if we exercise the constraints Jesus obviously did, then we too will be okay! God bless you for hearing me out on this very controversial issue.

ARTICLE 11

Are You a Re-gifting Christian?

Re-gifting is the new age craze for many people at Christmas time each year. Re-gifting is simply receiving a gift that one might not want and / or feel they have any use for, then passing that gift on to someone else. This act is under the guise of giving the gift as if it was a new gift purchased by the giver to someone the giver feels will appreciate, need, and use. Re-gifting has become so popular that in the USA, "<u>National Re-gifting Day</u>" is celebrated on December 18th.

When I think about Christmas as it relates to the practice of re-gifting, I think about God's greatest gift to humankind, His Son, Jesus Christ! This gift was not, is not, and will not be capable of being re-gifted! God gives this wonderful gift to everyone, and as I have heard many Baptist preachers say, "I don't believe you heard me," this wonderful gift is given to everyone, whether one wants to accept it or NOT!

This is an excellent place for us to contemplate whether we as Christians, re-gift any of the gifts the Lord has given us. To that end, let us look at the basic definition of what a gift is.

A gift may be defined as: a thing [of value] given willingly to someone [without the expectation of] payment; a present [such as a Birthday or] a Christmas gift. Wow! God has given us a gift in His son that came with no expectation of payment. Another definition of a gift is a natural ability or talent. Respectfully, I suggest there are no natural abilities or talents, as all abilities and talents are derived from God, whether we chose to use them or not. Do you know someone who would perhaps be a great teacher, a Sunday School teacher? Do you know someone with tremendous gifts of singing and / or playing an instrument who could bless the Lord with their gift but does not? Should we all not live a righteous life where we have faith in His Word and govern ourselves accordingly?

So, what are the gifts God gives us that we might re-gift to someone else to assist the Lord building His Kingdom while simultaneously blessing someone else?

Romans chapter 12, I Corinthians 12, and Ephesians 4, all address the Spiritual Gifts that God gives us. Romans 12:4-8 in the NIV translation of the Bible reads, "[4] For just as each of us has one body with many members, and these members do not all have the same function, [5] so in Christ we, though many, form one body, and each member belongs to all the others. [6] We have different gifts, according to the grace given to each of us. If your gift is prophesying, then prophesy in accordance with your faith; [7] if it is serving, then serve; if it is teaching, then teach; [8] if it is to encourage, then give encouragement; if it is giving, then give generously; if it is to lead, do it diligently; if it is to show mercy, do it cheerfully." I Corinthians 12:1, 4-11 in the NIV translations speaks to the Spiritual gifts where it reads, "1 Now about the gifts of the Spirit, brothers and sisters, I do not want you to be uninformed. ...

[4] There are different kinds of gifts, but the same Spirit distributes them. [5] There are different kinds of service, but the same Lord. [6] There are different kinds of working, but in all of them and in everyone it is the same God at work.

⁷ Now to each one the manifestation of the Spirit is given for the common good. ⁸ To one there is given through the Spirit a message of wisdom, to another a message of knowledge by means of the same Spirit, ⁹ to another faith by the same Spirit, to another gifts of healing by that one Spirit, ¹⁰ to another miraculous powers, to another prophecy, to another distinguishing between spirits, to another speaking in different kinds of tongues,[a] and to still another the interpretation of tongues.[b] ¹¹ All these are the work of one and the same Spirit, and he distributes them to each one, just as he determines." Ephesians 4:1-6 from again the NIV translation reminds us of the spiritual gifts that the Lord gives us FREELY! "1 As a prisoner for the Lord, then, I urge you to live a life worthy of the calling you have received. ² Be completely humble and gentle; be patient, bearing with one another in love. ³ Make every effort to keep the unity of the Spirit through the bond of peace. ⁴ There is one body and one Spirit, just as you were called to one hope when you were called; ⁵ one Lord, one faith, one baptism; ⁶ one God and Father of all, who is over all and through all and in all."

The Lord provides each of us with gifts that He wants us to use to glorify Him and His Divine purpose. Through our good works we might serve as an icon or a lighthouse of faith. Throughout my travels, I have seen lighthouses in New England and am reminded that their sole purpose is to guide ships entering a port to a safe harbor, a safe haven. If we were to use our Spiritual Gifts, we too might lead lost souls through good times and bad times just as a lighthouse guides ships on a quiet, sunny, clear day as well as on a stormy, dark night safely into port. However, I know I am not alone on the issue that maybe we do not want the Spiritual gifts God has provided us due to the attendant responsibilities that come with them. Hmm, maybe I do not want to be an icon or lighthouse for the Lord!

I have several friends who have shared with me how they struggle with their gifts of leading, caring for, and teaching God's people. I know it is an awesome, tiring, and exasperating job to have to share the blessings of our God given gifts with others. Maybe, however, I might re-gift my God given gift to another believer! How might I do this?

If I possess the gift of wisdom, can I re-gift it to others showing them how to make good decisions? If my gift is giving, could I re-gift this gift by being known as a generous giver without boasting about how much I give and how often, as the Pharisee's of old did in front of the Temple? If my gift is music and I do not want to be in the choir or have any desire of being the choir director, could I not re-gift my musical talents and abilities to someone in the choir or the choir director to improve the direction and individual talents of the choir? If your gift is teaching, could you re-gift your teaching gift by suggesting books, such as Bible Dictionaries, Commentaries, Concordances, etc. to those who have the desire to teach but who do not possess your level of teaching expertise?

I was a Computer Programmer for many years. Computer logic has a major component called a Conditional Statement, also known as an IF ... THEN ... ELSE [Otherwise] Statement. With this concept in mind, IF God has blessed you with a gift, THEN use that gift to glorify God, ELSE re-gift that gift to another Believer to further the DIVINE purpose of ALMIGHTY GOD! Enough said?

ARTICLE 12

Are You on God's Team or Satan's Team?

Satan and his minions have gone into overdrive in many of the churches today. There are almost as many scandals in our churches as there are in politics on the national and local levels. Satan's goal is to impede, subdue, and if possible, destroy the good works performed by many well-meaning congregants in the Houses of God. However, some of these congregants are unwittingly playing on Satan's team. While they may come to church and work in a ministry regularly, dressed in what they have convinced themselves and want others to believe is the uniform and armor of Jesus Christ's team, their actions make them unwitting traitors and key players, or should I say, "Most Valuable Players" on Satan's team. Their actions make them inimical, that is, a devoted and extremely hostile enemy of the Trinity!

We must understand at this point that a team is a group of people working toward a common goal. In order for the team to be successful, every team member must be dedicated to the proposition of working cooperatively, whether their goal is focused on a sport, political, socio-economic, or religious goal, etc. Each team member must have a specific skill set in regards to assigned roles and responsibilities. These skill sets must be consistently executed with the goal of perfection by each team member. Think here for a moment about the cooperation and perfection required of each member of a successful orchestra. Each member must play their assigned instrument in harmony with every other member, or there will be an unpleasant combination of musical notes.

The Bible clearly tells us that both God's primary team and Satan's primary team have an equal number of team members. However, each team member on Satan's team has a lesser skill set and power than that of God's team member. Too often, we ascribe too much power to Satan and his team while in actuality we are the culprits, the evildoers, evoking our will over God's will in our lust for power, status, money, etc.! Who was it that said, *"The devil made me do it"*? We know that God's primary team consists of God the Father, Jesus the Son, and the Holy Spirit (The Holy Trinity). Each member of God's team operates with a specific and divine role, in their specific position, like the players on a sports team. Satan's team (the unholy Trinity), also consists of three primary members each playing a specific role opposite the members of God's team. Satan's team consists of Satan who opposes God, the Anti-Christ who opposes Jesus, and the False Teachers and Prophets who oppose the Holy Spirit. Three is God's number of Divine completion, perfection and resurrection. These two teams are as equal in power and skill sets as an NBA team playing the state High School championship basketball team in any given state in the U. S. of A! Both teams have an equal number of players, each assigned to a specific role on their respective team, but there is a greater degree of talent that exists on one team (God's team) than that which exists on the opposing team (Satan's team).

So, what are the reasons behind the escalating levels of disunity and discord in our churches today? Are there any historical precedents for such heinous conduct by some people who profess to love the Lord but whose actions are diametrically opposed to God's will in His houses of worship? First, let us look at a historical and Biblical example of Christian disunity that led to disastrous results!

According to any major source of Jewish history, the ancient Israelites engaged the Roman empire in what came to be known as the Jewish Wars that occurred between 66 A.D. and 70 A. D. Most of the battles in the Jewish Wars were fought in or around the Holy city, Jerusalem. The Jewish historian, Josephus (aka Flavius Josephus), is probably our most accurate and reliable source for understanding how infighting amongst God's people aided and abetted the work of Satan's team. (Please see: The Works of Josephus: Translated by William Whiston, (The Wars of the Jews: Book 5-6, pages 664-726).

During a speech here in Detroit on November 10, 1963, Malcolm X stated,

"Of all our studies, history is best qualified to reward our research. And when you see that you've got problems, all you have to do is examine the historic method used all over the world by others who have problems similar to yours. And once you see how they got theirs straight, then you know how you can get yours straight."

One of the greatest Biblical examples we might look at as an example of similar events producing similar results of disunity in the church is the second Siege of Jerusalem in 70 AD. The 1st Siege of Jerusalem occurred in 597 BC, when King Nebuchadnezzar ransacked the entire city and its Temple, placed the Israelites in bondage, and carried them to Babylon. This first siege led to the diaspora or dispersal of the Israelites by the Babylonians under the rule of King Nebuchadnezzar.

In 66 AD, the Israelites operated as diverse and sometimes hostile groups, one against the other, in a fight to overthrow their Roman oppressors, mostly using guerilla tactics. This division and disunity amongst the Israelites stemmed from men in each clan wanting to be the leader of the entire Jewish army. However, if these men could not be the ultimate military leader, they opted to be the leader of their own small family army. Sound familiar?

This war came to a boiling point in 70 AD, when the Roman general, Titus (*not to be confused with Paul's son in the ministry, Titus*), besieged the city of Jerusalem. There was internal warfare inside the walls of Jerusalem because there were two major military leaders among the Jews besieged in Jerusalem. People basically took sides and established what we might call cliques to support their favorite Jewish leader in control of a particular area or "side" of Jerusalem, God's Holy City. Sound familiar?

The two main Jewish military leaders were Simon and John. Each man controlled a portion of the city of Jerusalem and had a large military following. These groups who fought against the Romans and against the forces of the other Jewish leader, killed Romans and Jews opposing them and impeded the worship of God in the Temple due to their infighting on God's sacred ground. This infighting was so intense and so devastating that Josephus, the Jewish historian wrote, "But although they had grown wiser at the first onset the Romans made upon them, this lasted but a while, for they returned to their former madness, and separated one from another, and fought it out, and did all the besiegers could desire them to do; for they never suffered anything worse from the Romans than they made each other suffer, nor was there any misery endured by the city after these men's actions that could be esteemed new!" Sound familiar? It sounds like an "East Side versus West Side" mentality in God's House to me! And unfortunately, this mentality exists in God's Houses of worship today!

The disunity in the besieged city of Jerusalem led to the complete destruction of this Holy city. The Romans just retreated and surrounded the city, allowed the Israelites to enter the city for Passover services, and when supplies ran low, the Jewish factions fought it out, one against the other to the death. All the Romans had to do was walk in and take over, which they did, destroying the city and dispersing its occupants. Satan claimed the VICTORY!

So what do we do about this disunity in God's House? We should consult the scriptures for our answer.

I am of the opinion that if my brother or sister in the church sins against me while I am attempting to do the Lord's work, then they are sinning against the entire body of Christ. With that in mind, we may want to consult Matthew 18:15 (NIV) where a heading entitled, "Dealing With Sin in the Church" reads:

[15] "If your brother or sister sins go and point out their fault, just between the two of you. If they listen to you, you have won them over. [16] But if they will not listen, take one or two others along, so that 'every matter may be established by the testimony of two or three witnesses. [17] If they still refuse to listen, tell it to the church; and if they refuse to listen even to the church, treat them as you would a pagan or a tax collector.

We should also appreciate the advice the Apostle Paul gave his protégé, Timothy, in II Timothy 2:23-24 (NIV), which states, "Don't have anything to do with foolish and stupid arguments, because you know they produce quarrels. And the Lord's servant must not quarrel; instead, he must be kind to everyone, able to teach, not resentful."

The leader within the Body of Christ, then must be the primary Change Agent to stop and / or address any disunity in the House of God and bring about unity within the Body of Christ. The Pastor of a church then must be prepared to admonish malcontents and members of cliques of their harmful ways and be prepared to chastise them in a Godly way if necessary.

The Apostle Paul had many apropos words of advice on how to deal with such situations and people that cause disunity in the Body of Christ.

In Philippians 4:2 (NIV), Paul wrote, "I plead with Euodia and I plead with Syntyche to agree with each other in the Lord." In II Timothy 2:14 (NIV) Paul states, "Keep reminding them of these things. Warn them before God against quarreling about words. It is of no value and only ruins those who listen." In Titus 3:10-11 Paul wrote, "Warn a divisive person once, and then warn him a second time. After that, have nothing to do with him. You may be sure that such a man is warped and sinful; he is self-condemned." Finally, in Titus 2:15-3:1, Paul wrote "These, then, are the things you should teach. Encourage and rebuke with all authority. Do not let anyone despise you. Remind the people to be subject to rulers and authorities, to be obedient, to be ready to do whatever is good." Most of Paul's advice was to the church leaders of his day, but it is also valuable advice to those of us who want to promote harmony, a virtual esprit de corps in the churches of today.

Eldridge Cleaver (the 1960s social commentator, political writer, political activist and an early leader of the

Black Panther Party founded in Oakland, CA., in 1966 by Huey P. Newton and Bobby Seale) once said, "If you are not a part of the solution, you are a part of the problem." The choice in my mind is an easy one! I have chosen to be on God's team to be part of God's solution to the ills that adversely impact upon us, and I am trying to gain, sustain, and maintain a starting position on God's team! What about you?

ARTICLE 13

Do You Realize Who You Have in Your Corner When in the Heat of Battle Against Satan?

As Christians we have read scripture that readily suggests that we are engaged in a protracted, incessant, and never ending war with Satan and his numerous minions! But we all more than likely remember a true story about an individual, group, or team that conquered insurmountable odds to achieve an unexpected, amazing victory.

One such well known biblical story is that of the battle of David and Goliath. David was a simple shepherd boy, and Goliath was a fearsome and fearless Philistine warrior who was at least nine feet tall. The Lord loved David, however, and protected him from harm. The Lord equipped David with an invisible armor that neither the mighty Philistines nor David's countrymen could see. We all know the story, and hopefully we have an appreciation of what David did before he engaged Goliath in battle. David only had a simple sling or slingshot, which was the typical defense weapon used by the ancient Israelites to ward off their enemies. More importantly, as sheep herders and shepherds the sling was used to kill wild animals that viewed sheep as prey! Before meeting Goliath, David went to a nearby stream and picked up five smooth stones. One may ask why he did this. Was David unsure of his skill and accuracy with the slingshot? Was David a little concerned that the Lord might not protect him as he fought this battle that would ultimately determine the future of his nation and people? No, it was David's faith in God that told him to select the five smooth stones because David and the other Israelites knew that Goliath had four brothers who were also giants!

Let us not forget that none of David's family or the men of his tribe even considered having him face Goliath. It was the prophet Samuel who instructed the Israelites to send David out to meet Goliath.

The prophet, Samuel, knew that God had a plan that went farther than just the defeat of the Philistines. David, the shepherd boy, was an integral part of God's future plan for the nation of Israel! Please remember, David was Jesse's eighth son and eight is God's number for new birth, new creation, and new beginnings!

David selected the five smooth stones because he heard that Goliath had four brothers and he wanted to be prepared in the event this family of giants were to attempt to attack him to avenge the death of their brother.

David, the eighth son of Jesse, was to usher into existence Israel's new birth, new creation and a new beginning after he slew Goliath!

This is the type of assurance, the type of faith we modern day Christians must have as we meet the Goliaths in our lives on a daily basis. These contemporary Goliaths come in the form of a Goliath called inadequate finances, or poor health, or deteriorating family and personal relationships. And let us not forget the Goliath of bereavement. This Goliath devastates us through our mourning for a loved one who has made their transition from this life to the next. We need to vigorously fight off this Goliath because he will have us question why the Lord took such a good and devoted believer while there are so many cheating, deceitful, and evil people walking around flaunting their evil deeds right in God's face. They are inimical to Jesus Christ!

Yes, Goliath may have been slain by David centuries ago, but the essence of his kinfolk comes knocking on our door each and every day wanting to take us out. It behooves us as Christians to be like David and prepare for the destructive intrusions of Satan's minions, the Goliaths we face, by staying in prayer. I love what one of this country's greatest philosophers, Satchel Paige, once said, "Don't pray when it's raining if you can't pray when the sun is shining." Why do we sometimes wait until Goliath and his Philistine cronies have encamped themselves on our doorstep before we pray? Why do we wait until someone else comes to our assistance when we could have averted some of our Goliaths by taking better care of ourselves! We need to be vigilant and ward off those Goliaths that attack us physically. Why do we not have our slingshot ready to fling a smooth stone at the Goliath who is preventing us from staying in meaningful and blessed relationships? Why do we let the Goliath of failed marriages block our view of the person the Lord has in store for us? Why can't we live within the means God has provided rather than not being good stewards of the money God blessed us with? I love what the Apostle Paul had to say on the subject in Philippians 4:11-13, "[11] I am not saying this because I am in need, for I have learned to be content whatever the circumstances. [12] I know what it is to be in need, and I know what it is to have plenty. I have learned the secret of being content in any and every situation, whether well fed or hungry, whether living in plenty or in want. [13] I can do all this through Him who gives me strength."

We just might want to look at the Goliath's in our lives sent by Satan as opposed to those Goliath's we inadvertently created!

There are some scriptures that even suggest that we put on the armor of God as we wage war against the Prince of Darkness and his unlimited warriors. I liken these scriptures to one of my favorite sports, boxing.

I was born and raised in Louisville, Kentucky. Louisville is also the home of the "Greatest Of All Time (GOAT)" prize fighter, Muhammad Ali. In most of the fights that Ali had after turning professional, he always had three "corner men" that he heavily relied on. George Bundini Brown, "float like a butterfly, sting like a bee, rumble young man rumble," Ali's motivator, Dr. Ferdie Pacheo, his fight Doctor and cut man who tended to Ali's wounds during the one minute break between rounds, and Angelo Dundee, Ali's most capable trainer who got Ali in shape for all his fights, no matter the opponent.

We too have three entities in our corner as we face Satan's team each and every day. We are blessed to be motivated, healed, and taught the way of God by our three corner men, God the father, Jesus the Son, and the Holy Spirit/Ghost. If we would only listen to our heavenly corner men as Ali did his corner men during his reign as a heavyweight champion, we would be as successful as Ali in terms of our wins verses losses against Satan.

The words of Jesus found in the gospel of John, 15:5-9 are ever so apropos at this juncture. Jesus said, "5 "I am the vine; you are the branches. If you remain in me and I in you, you will bear much fruit; apart from me you can do nothing. 6 If you do not remain in me, you are like a branch that is thrown away and withers; such branches are picked up, thrown into the fire and burned. 7 If you remain in me and my words remain in you, ask whatever you wish, and it will be done for you. 8 This is to my Father's glory, that you bear much fruit, showing yourselves to be my disciples.

Like Ali, let us play our assigned role and let our great and talented corner men do their jobs as we fight the minions of Satan in our lives. If we do our part in maintaining our faith in the Lord, to God goes all the glory!

I know what I am suggesting is not easy, but if you could see what all successful boxers go through to prepare for a fight, you would understand why they would willingly admit, "It ain't easy, but the rewards of victory are great!"

Let us stay focused on the Lord, and our victory over Satan is certain!

ARTICLE 14

Are You Willing to Forfeit Your Life for A Godly Cause?

I remember reading that Dr. Martin Luther King stated, "a man who has not found something to die for is not fit to LIVE!"

That is an awesome, insightful, and profound statement that should immediately guide us to reflect on and question ourselves as Christians.

Are we willing to die for the Lord, the Lord who gave His life on the Cross so we might have eternal life? I know and believe that there are people we might die for. The people I believe I would willingly die for being a very distinct and minute group of wonderful people who the Lord has truly blessed me to be in my life! Do not look at me like I am selfish or an egomaniac as we both know that the number of people you would WILLINGLY forfeit your life for could be counted on one hand not using your thumb and pinky finger. I also believe that we might be willing to die to preserve our lifestyle in this capitalistic, egocentric, and conspicuously materialistic society. There are some who accept jobs where they know their life will be on the line in order to protect and defend the "American Way of Life." I even believe that some of my acquaintances would forfeit their lives to save the life of their pets! Please do not hate me for what I am about to say, but, "sorry Fido, Rover etc." If some potential life threatening situation arises where I have to choose your life or mine, my vote will be cast in favor of my survival. I do, however, promise to ensure you get an elaborate funeral in the doggie cemetery. I am just being REAL!!! But my question again is are we willing to forfeit our lives for God?

The Muslims are renowned for their outstanding loyalty, pronounced faith, extreme devotion and dedication to, and willingness to die for their religious beliefs! We do not have to search ancient history to find evidence that they are willing to give up their lives for their beliefs. Does 911 prove and substantiate my assertion?

So honestly, Brother James, are you willing to die as a Martyr for God the Father, Jesus the Son, and the Holy Spirit? Well, honestly, my friend, NO, I would not, as some Buddhist Monks did during the height of the Vietnam War, douse myself with a flammable fluid and set myself ablaze to prove I am a REAL Christian with an undying faith in the Lord. No, I would not enroll in a pilot training class with my focus and only objective being to learn the processes of takeoffs and not landing so I could pilot a huge airplane into a skyscraper to get to heaven quicker and take hundreds if not thousands of innocent people along for the ride. Even Greyhound Bus Lines and every airline, irrespective of its size, gives those who purchased a ticket to be transported to a specific destination the option of a scheduled and accepted departure date and time and date of return. So, if I were to give up my life to be with the Lord, I would make that trip alone! I may not be willing on a moment's notice to forfeit my life for the Lord, but I am willing to DIE to the Sin in my life! I am willing to exterminate the sins of my life as the Apostle Paul addresses in Romans 6:1- 4 where the NIV reads thusly, "[1] What shall we say, then? Shall we go on sinning so that grace may increase? [2] By no means! We are those who have died to sin; how can we live in it any longer? [3] Or don't you know that all of us who were baptized into Christ Jesus were baptized into his death?

[4] We were therefore buried with him through baptism into death in order that, just as Christ was raised from the dead through the glory of the Father, we too may live a new life. "Yes, I am willing to kill the sins of the flesh those carnal desires within me that might ultimately destroy me as Paul wrote in Galatians 5:24 Amplified Bible (AMP) "[24] And those who belong to Christ Jesus have crucified the sinful nature together with its passions and appetites."

And yes, I am willing to take a lethal Spiritual overdose of FAITH in the Lord that would kill the sinful nature within me. It is worthwhile to consult the Apostle Paul, the Apostle to the Gentiles once again, who in 2 Corinthians 5:17 New Living Translation (NLT) wrote,

[17] This means that anyone who belongs to Christ has become a new person. The old life is gone; a new life has begun!

I am willing to forfeit my sinful nature, my sinful life, so I might live eternally in Heaven! Becoming a New Being in God's eyes is definitely more trying, more physically painful, more emotionally challenging and demanding than a quick, physical death because it takes a longer period of time to go through a day by day death to Sin.

I feel it improper for me to ask anyone to do something that I am not willing to do. Are you willing to forfeit your sinful life, not physical death, but a death to the life you live that is creating a chasm between you and God's plan for you? Are you willing to die as the process of baptism symbolizes to become a NEW You, a dedicated Christian in the truest meaning of the term? Are you then willing to die of SELF so that the Lord may use you for His Divine purpose? Are you with me on being crucified, then set on fire spiritually for the Lord, or will you live a life chasing some elusive sinful dream to be rich, popular, powerful and famous in the world? Where are you in your protracted fight against succumbing to your sinful nature? Again, I ask, are you ready, willing, and able to die to the SIN in your life? Please give this interrogatory a lot of thought! Serious thought!

ARTICLE 15

Are You a Spoiled Christian?

Words and their attendant usage are very important! Some people use words with the sole intent to aggrandize themselves or to gain the favor of those they feel are important. I use the words "fake" and "sycophant" to describe such people! Others use words to impress others with their false, perpetrated intellect. I use the word pseudo-intellectual to describe such folks. Others may use specific words and an overuse and abuse of slang words without realizing or caring how harmful the words might be to the recipient. I use words such as callous, boorish, haters, and I love this word, lumpen, which means low class or totally devoid of any sophistication, to describe the people of this ilk! There is an old adage, "words can oftentimes be more harmful than fists!" Have you ever used a word or words that was/were completely misunderstood by the recipient?

    Many years ago I wrote a six page letter to a beautiful, intelligent, African American female, with whom I was enamored. In the midst of the letter I stated that I was unable to truly express my feelings for her because I am an "introvert." Now, please remember that the letter was six pages in length; however, she focused her attention on my use of the word "introvert" which she understood to mean that I WAS EGOCENTRIC and SELFISH. I was shocked, I thought everyone who used the term introvert or introverted knew it meant shy! Obviously, there are very few words in the English language that have only one definition, and much to my dismay, I learned her use of the word had very negative connotations. Woe be unto me as she responded by saying she could not and would not relate to someone who was self-absorbed, selfish, and egocentric.

I use this example to illustrate how a speaker or writer might use words to imply one thing while the recipient, the listener or reader might infer a totally different meaning and consequently, a distorted point of view! Recently, two people in a barbershop had a discussion I overheard and enjoyed about the use of the word, "SPOILED."

Have you ever heard someone say, "His or her children are spoiled brats"? Have you ever heard someone say, "He spoiled his wife on her birthday"? Or have you ever said, "I spoiled myself this weekend because I deserve it"?

Yes, we all have heard others or ourselves use the word "spoiled" in this context. So, I ask at this juncture, are you a spoiled Christian?

Let us look at the true meaning that should be assigned or associated with the word "spoiled."

To spoil means to diminish or destroy the value or quality of something. You would not want to drink spoiled milk or eat spoiled food, right? You would not want someone to spoil your evening when you had intended to rest by keeping your telephone conversation with those same old issues you have gone over and over again. Would you want someone to spoil your favorite movie by their "talking loud but saying nothing"? Am I wrong?

Some synonyms of spoil are: harm, ruin, destroy, invalidate, mar, damage, impair, blemish. None of these words offer any positive meanings. These words are definitely devoid of grace and mercy. They all deny the promise of a productive future! I ask again, given the definition provided, are you a SPOILED CHRISTIAN?

As a Christian, do you possess socially, and more importantly, any Christian redeemable qualities?

Are you so spoiled as a Christian that you are the only focus of your limited universe? Do you care so much about the issues and adversities confronting your neighbors that you could win the "Good Samaritan of the Year Award"? Are you so spoiled that every time you enter the Body of Christ, allegedly to worship, your fellow congregants avoid you as if you were the carrier of any dreaded and life-threatening disease or reeked of spoiled milk, stale beer, and spoiled fish?

I firmly believe that in every situation there is the equivalent of a litmus test! Can you, will you pass the Lord's litmus test of your demonstrated love for Him, His Word, and His People? Or, are you truly a spoiled Christian, one that the Lord should ignore as He did the ancient Israelites for 400 years between Malachi and Matthew? Too many Christians of today have a false sense of entitlement where they only call on God when they want but not necessarily need anything! Spoiled Christians think that God should consider them as the center of His universe. However, these spoiled Christians should consider the words found in Romans 2:11 where Paul wrote, "For God does not show favoritism." The Apostle Peter reiterates this theme when he stated in Acts 10:34, "**I now realize how true it is that God does not show favoritism**"

God's promise to take care of our needs is not exclusive to the Spoiled Christians and the proof of this is found in two profound scriptures. The NIV translation of God's Word speaks to us on this issue where Jesus said, "25 "**Therefore I tell you, do not worry about your life, what you will eat or drink; or about your body, what you will wear. Is not life more than food, and the body more than clothes"? The other scripture that comes to mind when I think about spoiled Christians only calling upon the Lord when they need something is mentioned in Philippians 4:19 NIV translation that reads thusly, "[19] And my God will meet all your needs according to the riches of his glory in Christ Jesus".

Can the Lord count on you every day to do His Divine Will, or are you so ruined by your self-imposed selfishness that He cannot use you to work diligently in His vineyard? Can you be counted on to always try to do the righteous and Christian thing in every situation, or are you so impaired that you cannot clearly see the road ahead of you to attain salvation? Do you always do what you want, finding the need for the Lord to constantly rescue you from yet another self-made debacle? Are you in a self-induced and self-manufactured quagmire because you are a Spoiled Christian so marred, damaged, and blemished in terms of your demonstration of non-Christian acts and speech that all who encounter you see you only as a SPOILED CHRISTIAN? Trust me, I have asked these questions of myself!

Do you fit the thought provoking description of a Spoiled Christian found in 2 Timothy 3:2-4, "[2] People will be lovers of themselves, lovers of money, boastful, proud, abusive, disobedient to their parents, ungrateful, unholy, [3] without love, unforgiving, slanderous, without self-control, brutal, not lovers of the good, [4] treacherous, rash, conceited, lovers of pleasure rather than lovers of God (NIV)".

Respectfully, why do you not "marinate" on this interrogatory as to whether or not you are a SPOILED CHRISTIAN for a few minutes? Okay, time is up. What say you"?

ARTICLE 16

Will God Allow You to Enter The Gates of Heaven with a "D" Average?

No matter how far you were blessed to go in school, you would have to agree with the following grading system: an "A" means excellence in achievement; a "B" means above average achievement; a "C" means average achievement; a "D" means below average but minimally passing achievement; and an "E" or "F" means failure in that given subject. The question that now arises is, "when it comes to serving God, are we putting forth the effort to get an "A," or are we satisfied and content to meet the minimum requirements and perhaps enter the gates of Heaven with a "D" average for our Christian efforts?

Recently, I was sitting in one of my doctor's offices and was very impressed by all the Degrees, Diplomas, and Certificates of academic achievement that adorned his office walls. As I waited to be seen, I casually looked at all of them and noticed they had one thing in common. Each of them had language that showed that the doctor had "Satisfactorily Completed," or "Successfully Met," or "Completed the Required Hours of Study" to be a recipient of that particular degree. Now, let us reflect on, or as they say in my old neighborhood, "let's marinate on that for a moment!" "Satisfactorily Completed," or "Successfully Met," or "Completed the Required Hours of Study," means that my doctor, who is prescribing me medications, operating on me, and / or referring me to another doctor who is a specialist, may have graduated from Medical School with a "D" average! He passed, but where in his class was he by academic achievement compared to his peers? There was absolutely no verbiage in any of the degrees mounted on his office walls that said, "He Mastered," or "He Excelled," or "He Surpassed," the requirements for graduation! Again, all of his degrees basically implied that he just made a "passing grade." At West Point, the Air Force, and Naval Academies, they always publish where the future military leaders of this nation graduated in their graduating class. These graduates will boast, "I was first in my class," or "I was fifteenth in my class," but we never hear who was last in his or her graduating class at these military institutions of higher military tactical learning. However, what we must understand is that under certain stressful and wartime conditions the person at the bottom of his or her graduating class may be placed in a critical position of leadership. They could conceivably be faced with making life and death decisions that could adversely affect the lives of our sons and daughters, sisters and brothers, etc. Scary huh? Also scary is not knowing where the anesthesiologist who puts me under before surgery or the doctor who is operating on me could have passed, perhaps just barely with a "D" average. I am confident that most health care professionals are proficient in their given medical specialty, but I am just using them in my example.

Does God want the least, a "D" effort from us, or does He want and should He justifiably expect the best, "A" effort from us? Does God care that we will sit in the rain overnight to get tickets to see a celebrity concert, or a sports playoff event, or even to be first in line to get the latest pair of Nikes or the newest iPhone? All of these events take an "A" effort in preparation to withstand the elements necessary to sit and/or stand outside overnight without the creature comforts of home, most notably the access to and use of indoor plumbing.

Does the Lord say, "I love you so much and I do so much for you that it is okay for you to only show me an "A" effort when you need something from Me"? Therefore, is it not always okay to be on time for social club meetings, sporting events, our jobs, and have a nearly perfect work record, but then be so habitually late to church that those who come on time say, "oh, it must be 11:25am because Brother and Sister "Late-As-Usual" just came in! Too many Christians believe that the minimal requirement to enter the kingdom of heaven, espoused in Romans 10:9, *"If you declare with your mouth, "Jesus is Lord," and believe in your heart that God raised him from the dead, you will be saved. (NIV)"* is all that is required to get into heaven. God truly expects from us more than just a confession of our faith in Him and His Son, Jesus Christ. However, there are those who feel that as long as they believe in Jesus, they do not have to participate in any church ministry, contribute generously to the church, or fellowship in their home based church. They would rather choose to watch a church service on TV. And, of course, there are those who rarely demonstrate Christian conduct and values on their jobs, in their families, or neighborhoods that would create an environment conducive for others to want to become a Christian. These "D" average folks are not only manifesting worldly lifestyles but are also totally immersed in the world. So, why would a non-believer want to become a Christian when they see those of us with a "D" average mentality acting, talking, and thinking just like them?

I believe God has certain expectations of each of us, and His expectations are that we will ALWAYS put forth an "A" effort. I believe God does not care if we get a "B" or a "C" in our efforts to do His Will, as long as we sincerely put forth an "A" effort. Just as with most things in life, you will make a few mistakes along the way, but as long as you are striving for perfection in your Christian walk, you are on the right course! I know I am not alone as a former student who worked hard and diligently to get an "A" in a particular class, only missing a couple of questions on a test, or having the paper I wrote graded a "B," but realizing in my heart that putting forth the "A" effort was what mattered most. I gave that class all the energy and time I had to pass, and that is what we must do to please God. We must always try to give Him our very best! We must always strive to give God the same level of effort as we do worldly things. It is only FAIR?

ARTICLE 17

Are You Going THROUGH Something???

The word through automatically implies five situations and/or conditions. These five situations and/or conditions are: movement, a starting and ending point, distance, time, and a destination.

Without ever having met you or having any personal knowledge of you, I can say with a great deal of certainty that you are going through something! We are all going through something! No one can live in this modern era and be immune to all trials and tribulations!

It is virtually impossible to live in this contemporary world and not be burdened with some spiritual, health, financial, emotional and/or relationship issue or issues.

We must all understand, however, that God never tempts us but will test us. He will test us by taking us "through" some situations we might feel are unfair and unwarranted. He may take us through some situations where we might feel we are being tested and do not understand. "Why me Lord, why me?"

Have you ever posed the question, "Why me, Lord?" to ALMIGHTY GOD? Honestly, I have! God might take us through some situations where we do not see a foreseeable end, a quick exit from our pain and suffering. Have you gone through a difficult divorce, death of a significant other, loss of a job, or been tormented by someone on the job? Have you fretted over such devastating issues with no possible positive resolution in sight, for only God knows how long? God only takes us through hardship and challenging times to make us stronger in our faith. Do you remember the beautiful lesson on faith manifested in the story of the trials and tribulations of Job?

Have you ever wondered if God might be ignoring or neglecting you as he takes you through SOMETHING? Please allow me to inform you that whether it's those we see and worship on TV reality shows, entertainers, or professional athletes, they are all going through something! Wealth, status, and fame are not the panacea against having turmoil, hardships, and stress in one's life. No one in this world is immune to or has received a supernatural inoculation against the trials and tribulations associated with having some situation that they are going through as a direct result of living in a capitalistic society!

The famed and exceedingly wealthy actor, Robin Williams, committed suicide. Jay Z and his sister-in-law Solange had an altercation on an elevator of a posh hotel that was shown to a worldwide audience. And, let us not forget all the professional athletes brought up on drug, alcohol, domestic violence, and abuse charges. Oh, I say again, it is sad to say, but money, status, and power are still no protection from God taking us through SOMETHING! No matter whether we are rich or poor, uneducated, well educated, or the epitome of success or failure in life, we are all going through something!

I am reminded of something I heard attributed to the rap artist, TI, who said, "Sometimes God will take us through Hell so he might get us to Heaven." That insightful statement waxed profoundly with me. What is the hell you are going through? Was any of it self-imposed? If you have health issues, do you intake things in your temple that led to your current health issues? I recently had a couple of relatives who made their transition to heaven because they smoked for many years. Most had not smoked in over 30 years, but their cause of death was attributed to long term abuse of tobacco. If your hell is financially generated, were you not a good steward of the monies that the Lord provided you and you tried to live a sirloin steak lifestyle on a bologna budget? Remember, God, at the very least, did give you a budget. If your hell is spawned by a relationship issue with a child, other family member, or someone of the opposite sex, did you follow the road map that God provides in his Holy Word for raising children, dealing with one's blood relations and in-laws, or His courting and marriage rules? Everything we need to know about avoiding many of the downfalls and obstacles we encounter in life are found in God's Holy Word!

All we need to do is to consult the words the Apostle Paul wrote to the church at Corinth, located at I Corinthians 13:4-8a (with "a" representing the first sentence in verse 8), "

4 Love is patient, love is kind. It does not envy, it does not boast, it is not proud. 5 It does not dishonor others, it is not self-seeking, it is not easily angered, and it keeps no record of wrongs. 6 Love does not delight in evil but rejoices with the truth. 7 It always protects, always trusts, always hopes, and always perseveres.

8 Love never fails (NIV).

Maybe this is an ideal place for us to walk through each of the five situations and/or conditions that I suggested the word "through" implies. I previously said that the word "through" automatically implies five situations and/or conditions. These five situations and/or conditions are:

movement, a starting and ending point, distance, time, and destination.

If we were to carefully analyze the situations we are going through, we would have to admit that there is some type of *movement* involved. We enter and exit a structure by moving through a door. While driving, we sometimes have to move through a tunnel. We move in and out of relationships without consulting the Lord before, during, and after the relationships end. We move the priority position that God once held in our lives to a position lower than that of some false preacher and teacher, a pimp in the pulpit, whom we have elevated to being our idol or god in our lives. We move our fellowship from one church to another looking for that perfect church because the congregation, we attend does not properly address the things we are spiritually going through! In this vein, we move like the ancient Greek philosopher, Diogenes, who was said to carry a lit lantern day and night in an endless and futile search to find an honest man. We move farther and farther away from the true word of God, opting to accept and practice such inane religious teachings as the prosperity gospel the plant a seed gospel, or the name it and claim it gospel because we believe these false gospels will deliver us from what we are going through, especially if we put more money into the collection plate.

Did Jesus, Paul, or any of the Apostles seek money from those they preached to so the generous giver would have riches here on earth? No, the Bible I read clearly indicates that the riches these venerable men spoke of were in Heaven, not necessarily here on earth!

I firmly believe that everything has a point of origin. Nothing, just happens. The "Big Bang Theory," the scientific explanation of how life as we know it began as opposed to the TV show, has no basis of truth. Everything in life has a *starting and ending point.* We are born, then we die! In many forms of racing, such as horse racing, track and field, and automobile racing, there is both a starting line and a finish line. However, God gives us, through His permissive will, the ability to choose reaching a finish line in hell or attaining salvation with our finish line found basking in the glory with the heavenly host found in heaven.

Life is a journey, and all journeys are comprised with the element of *distance.* We might consider the distance we travel in our Christian walk from the lack of knowledge to our understanding what it truly means to be saved. Some folks go on an emotional or a spiritual trip going the distance from the gates of hell to the gates of heaven! How many people do you know who made a spiritual journey that included the distance in their beliefs, similar to that made by Saul of Tarsus to become the Apostle Paul? How many people do you know who positively changed their lives, the path from hell to heaven abruptly after meeting Jesus? Saul of Tarsus went the distance, a virtual metamorphosis from being a man inimical to Christ to become the greatest apostle in the first century AD! Incidentally, Paul wrote over two-thirds of the New Testament. How many people do you know that you would not trust with your home, or would not trust enough to loan a few dollars? However, you now look at them with sincere respect as a result of a wonderful spiritual metamorphosis? These folks went the distance, a divinely inspired spiritual journey while God took them through something. They went the distance and answered the bell at the beginning of the twelfth and final and decisive round of their boxing match against the wiles of Satan. Again, they spiritually and emotionally went the distance and WON!

I am a huge boxing fan, and in the sweet science of boxing, there is a well used phrase of, "going the distance."

Now the distance alluded to here is not the distance of a road trip or airline flight; rather, it is the distance one endures to sustain and maintain oneself during the rigors of a twelve round, three minutes per round boxing match where the opponent is trying to knock them out. Well, sometimes God will test us by taking us through situations that test our mettle just so we will survive and come to at the end of the fight with Satan and his minions victorious.

There is another boxing term related to going the "distance," we need to explore here and that is the mandatory eight count. When one boxer is being pummeled by his opponent and appears to be unable to continue, the referee will temporarily stop the fight and give the distressed boxer a mandatory eight second period of relief to determine if the fight should stop or continue. I have seen many boxing matches where that mere eight seconds was enough time for the badly beaten boxer to regain his composure, continue the fight, and claim the victory!

Have you ever had the occasion where God was testing you? All may have seemed lost, but Jesus was your referee, and after giving you the mandatory eight count, were you able to fight your battle against tremendous odds and claim victory? I know I have! I know that if you only think about it, you would remember a situation where the Lord allowed Satan to test your spiritual mettle as God allowed Satan to test his servant, Job. At the beginning of the test, Job probably felt he had lost everything, but in actuality, he was both redeemed and restored by the Lord. Let us look at the meaning of one being redeemed and restored for our discussion.

Webster's definition of the word redeem is: to gain or regain possession of (something) in exchange for payment. Now let us look at this word from the concept of a Pawn Shop.

When someone places an item or items to be "pawned," the pawnshop owner will give that person a pawn or, a "redemption" ticket. So the story of Job teaches, in an analogous way, that God pawned His servant, Job, who incidentally had tremendous value to His arch rival, Satan, for a brief period. During that brief period, Satan did all he could do to persuade Job to curse God and deny the power God had over Satan. However, Job's faith was the key element of his value to God. It was Job's love of and indisputable faith in God that God allowed Satan to test Job. Job never wavered from worshipping God and Job maintained his faith in God while Satan took him *through* a multitude of challenges!

When Satan's harassment of Job failed, God exercised His Divine right to reclaim or REDEEM His servant and property from Satan. The question now arises, are you worthy of being redeemed by the Lord as a direct result of your Christian walk?

Webster's defines the word RESTORE in the following fashion: to bring back (a previous right, practice, custom, or situation); to reinstate. After Job's devastating personal losses, God did restore him in such a manner that he gained more than he lost. God knows what we are going through, and if we only maintain our faith in Him and have the "patience of Job," He will restore us to our former and better position in life. He will restore all that we lost that had an appreciable and intrinsic value to us as opposed to our worldly losses that we could have done without in the first place. All we need to do is to honor, trust, and obey God in all our thoughts, words, and deeds, and He will restore us in a supernatural fashion just as He did His servant, Job!

So, my friend, are your actions, thoughts, and speech significant enough to give the Lord an unassailable reason to bring restoration into your life?

Now, let us look at how God redeemed and restored His servant, Job.

The scripture clearly tells us the following:

After Job survived the onslaught of Satan's evil deeds, God blessed him to have more children. God also blessed Job to have double the amount of livestock, which made Job the wealthiest man in the "East." God also blessed Job with a long life, 140 years, where he lived long enough to see the next four generations of his family. God truly blessed, redeemed, and restored His servant beyond belief!

There are two major lessons we should observe and incorporate into our Christian walk contained within the story of Job. First, the story of Job teaches us to endure trials, testing, tribulations, and probation as we go through life. Have you ever heard the adage, "What does not kill us only makes us stronger"? Have you heard the terms persecution and martyrdom used in relation to the harsh treatment of professed Christians? Second, the story of Job is a story of redemption. Have you ever put something of value in Lay-Away then redeemed them at a later date? God allowed Satan to test Job's faith, and when Job passed the test with a perfect score, God redeemed him. I have learned from two great pastors in the Detroit metropolitan area two important lessons. Pastor Joseph Chatten, Pastor of Resurrection Mission Baptist Church, taught me that patience and faith in the Lord will help us surmount obstacles in life, even when everything seems hopeless. Pastor Jake Gaines, Pastor of Synagogue Baptist Church, taught me that God sometimes reverses the standard model of teaching. Normally, we are provided with a lesson and then given a test. However, God will give us the test, and therein lies the lesson. Job was faithful to the Lord and patient during his multitude of calamities. Job also passed his arduous test, and when he was redeemed by God, he appreciated the lesson.

So, we can discern that after Job faced his testing, trials, probation, and tribulations, he was fully redeemed by the Lord. The Lord did it for Job and He can do it for us. What we might be going through may be the Lord's way of preparing us for bigger and better things in this often arduous, long, and protracted journey called life.

We may conclude that the story of Job is initially a story of Job's trials, testing, tribulation, and probation. But, by being faithful and obedient, Job was redeemed and had all that he lost restored by Almighty God! This is an excellent "Life Lesson" in God's Word.

We all have heard the adage, "Time is money "*Time* is what plagues us the most as we go through something. There are devastating instances in our lives where we do not have enough time to resolve them. There are other adverse situations in this journey called life where we have too much time on our hands to reflect on those issues troubling us. The proof of my theory is that in those instances where we feel we did not have adequate time to deal with the issues we are going through, we can look back and truthfully say to ourselves, "If I had only used my head and spent time doing the right things in that given situation, I would have been okay and God would have truly blessed me!"

On the issue of having too much time as we go through a difficult situation, we often daydream. After daydreaming, we lose much needed time by fretting over those conditions outside of our control. Too often we go through what we choose to view as important issues to our social standing, our physical and financial health, and last, but not least, our spiritual growth! Yes, time is always present and must be handled properly as we go through something!

Have you ever been confronted and confused by adverse circumstances and had time to fix them, yet, decided to, "Lean on your own understanding" for a resolution? When was the first time you were faced with a perceived adverse issue that you took the time to call upon the Lord first, instead of putting on your "I can fix it tool belt and hard hat?" How much time do you spend calling or texting others to discuss your problems? How much time does it take to pray and simply say, "Lord, please help me"? I love what Pastor Gaines says on this issue of spending time with the Lord. Pastor Gaines asks, "What kind of relationship would you have with your significant other if you spent an equitable amount of time talking to them as you spend talking with the Lord"? Time spent in fervent prayer is of the essence when we are going through something! So, honestly, how much time do you spend in prayer instead of worrying when you are going through something?

Do you truly believe in the Lord's promise of salvation and eternal life? Are you truly "Sold Out" on Jesus, and accordingly have faith in the Lord's promise that your final *destination* is Heaven? Do you attempt to be a devout servant and a child of God by trying to live a sin-free life so you will avoid hell and wind up in heaven? Or, are you playing the Las Vegas odds by claiming to be a Christian who only attends church just in case there is a heaven? Respectfully, I ask, what is your desired destination in life? I have yet to meet anyone who has lived a sin-free life. Moreover, I have never met anyone who had, no regrets about past transgressions, made against others and, more importantly, transgressions against God. We all have made mistakes in life, but upon repenting, God forgives us and will allow us to enter heaven as our final destination. I have read accounts of people who, like the thief on the cross, confessed their sins and professed their belief in the Lord before taking their last breath. I realize you are acquainted with the story, but please indulge me as I share the relevant scripture on making heaven our final destination. Luke 23:42-43 states, [42] Then he said, "Jesus, remember me when you come into your kingdom." [43] Jesus answered him, "Truly I tell you, today you will be with me in paradise." The thief on the cross wanted his final destination to be heaven, so he made his deathbed profession (confessing and declaring or admitting ones past sins prior to their death, hence a deathbed profession/confession) of faith while making his deathbed confession of crimes committed! *If our final destination is truly heaven, it is never too late to repent. It is never too late to profess our love for Jesus as long as we have breath in our body.* We should, however, not wait to the last minute to profess our belief in Jesus. Please do not be like some folk in the club who wait for the "last call for alcohol." When I used to frequent the club scene, I noticed that when the last call for alcohol was made, many people ordered a double of whatever they were drinking. It occurred to me that their consumption of alcohol was such that they did not believe they would be able to get another drink tomorrow. Now is that any way to view one's life if their destination is heaven? Should we live a life knowing that one day Jesus will return to claim his own people, but think He will give us a notice akin to the last call for alcohol in the clubs? Or, should we live a life as righteous as possible so we will enter heaven when Jesus returns?

    I do not know about you, but I do realize that I have not lived a perfect Christian life, and I have many things for which I have repented. I also know that as I mature in my Christian walk, I would rather not wait until the day the clouds open up and there stands Jesus checking tickets for those whose destination is heaven and those whose destination is hell!

Yes, as the Rap artist TI wrote in the lyrics to one of his songs, "Sometimes God will take us through Hell to get us to Heaven!"

I find great comfort in the lyrics of the song , "My Testimony," by Reverend Marvin Sapp, "So glad I made it, I made it <u>through</u> In spite of the storm and rain, heartache and pain Still I'm declaring That I made it <u>through</u> See, I didn't lose Experience lost at a major cost But I never lost faith in you So if you see me cry, It's just a sign that I'm still alive I got some scars, but I'm still alive In spite of calamity, He still has a plan for me And it's working for my good And it's building my testimony I'm so glad I made it So glad I made it I made it <u>through</u>!"

I made it <u>thru</u> I made it <u>thru</u> Ooohhh, so if you see me cry It's just a sign that I'm, I'm still alive I got some scars, but I'm still alive in spite of calamity He still has a plan for me It's working out...

When we are going through something, it is imperative that we maintain our focus on the Lord. Too often we get impatient and try to remedy our adverse situation without consulting the Lord. I am not implying that we should just sit back and wait on the Lord. Rather, what I am suggesting is that in any challenging situation we should consult the best attorney, the best physician, the best mediator, and certainly the best counselor, no matter the issue in our lives before we make the moves we may later regret!

I hear you when you say that the Lord is moving a little too slowly in remedying your spiritual, emotional, health, financial, and moral issues you face on a daily basis. Yes, you might ask where the Lord is when others, to whom you have done no wrong make it their life's work to harass and demean you. Yes, the Lord may have us suffer what appears to be an unbearable health condition. The Lord may have us go through one bad relationship after another. He may have us go through a bankruptcy and have us start all over again financially. He may have us go through situations where our family and friends may forsake us. But, one day, like Job, He will restore us to our former position in life or immensely improve our current position in life. Please keep your focus on and trust in the Lord, and He Will guide you, protect you, and take you through whatever hardships you are going THROUGH!

ARTICLE 18

Are You a SINgle, Saved, and Satisfied Christian?

What do e-harmony.com, Match.com, Christiansmingles.com and countless other cyber dating websites all have in common? They are all emblematic of one undeniable fact, it is becoming increasingly more difficult to meet the person you dream of and fantasize about through conventional means. In many cultures arranged marriages are the rule of the day. In western cultures you will find the well-worn dictum that the best place to meet your future spouse is in church, at work, or at school. But, all these venues, avenues, and strategies are dismal failures for the vast majority of us.

Okay then, why not try joining a Christian SINgles ministry at your church if you are a Christian? Well, if one were to check out this mechanism to find your desired future spouse, look again. Most Christian SINgle ministries have one of two distinct focuses, each of which are absent of great success! There are Christian Single's ministries whose sole purpose is to unite unmarried SINgle Christian men with unmarried SINgle Christian women so they might one day marry and procreate, creating some little future Christians. The other Christian SINgle ministries are focused on uniting SINgle Christians so they may simply get together and engage in wholesome and entertaining activities, such as going to the movies, plays, concerts, sporting events, etc. with the potential of some of the Christian SINgle men and women uniting in Holy matrimony as a byproduct.

None of these practices, such as on-line dating services and church sponsored SINgles ministries seem to be working! How do I know this? Well, the amount of advertising for on-line dating services is increasing exponentially with new dating services specializing their focus on ethnic groups; cyber dating websites specifically oriented to lifestyle focused groups, such as farmersonly.com, singleparentmeet.com, dateacowboy.com, and elitesingles.com, and age specific, such as maturesinglesonly.com and ourtime.com etc. So, are you a single Christian in search of and in need of a wholesome, ordained, and blessed relationship with a Christian of the opposite sex? Do you want to fall madly and deeply in love with someone with whom you could be evenly yoked spiritually?

Please indulge me momentarily to share a poem of how two evenly yoked people should view one another. My poem is entitled, "How Is It That?"

How is it that...????

how is it that you can care for someone and love them so much that you could be 100's of miles apart and still feel their touch how is it that you could hold someone so near to your heart that you would yearn for them every second you were apart how is it that you always daydream of this special person you miss that you would walk, no, run a hundred miles to see them just for a hug and a kiss how is it that God has blessed, ordained you with a love from above that you'd have a nearly perfect relationship, totally saturated with love how is it that you trust one another so much when you are apart that doubts, suspicions, nor jealousy never enter your heart how is it that I have found the ultimate love, a love so true that is why I know that Almighty God blessed me by leading me to YOU!

Now, would it not be wonderful to be involved in a blessed relationship as outlined in this poem? But, most SINgle Christian folk are in a quandary trying to find that special someone of their dreams.

Christians, especially SINgle Christians, need LOVE, and they want to be engaged in a meaningful Christian relationship on a course in marriage. But, is that possible in our present day society? Is it necessary that you adhere to the word of God and be married in order to enjoy the pleasures of having children? If you do not want children, do you want to be married so you might experience the pleasure of having sex? Is abstinence the key to living a righteous SINgle Christian life? Oh, I love what the Last Poets wrote in one of their poems about the pleasure derived from having sex. *"Sex is pain, but it is good pain!"*

Please do not look at me all cross-eyed and crooked because of what I just implied! The Bible has an entire book, the Song of Songs/Solomon, that deals with the pleasure of sexual relations between a man and a woman! I sincerely pray that you look at this book in its entirety so you might know that the Bible covers every issue known to man, even sexual love.

If we were to look at the Song of Songs/Solomon 1:2-4a we would find the Queen of Sheba expressing her love for King Solomon and his sexual prowess when she stated, ²Let him kiss me with the kisses of his mouth— for your <u>love</u> is more delightful than <u>wine</u>. ³ Pleasing is the fragrance of your perfumes; your name is like perfume poured out. <u>No wonder the young women love you!</u> ⁴ Take me away with you—let us hurry! <u>Let the king bring me into his chambers.</u> Hmm, what do you think the Queen of Sheba's expectations were of King Solomon when they went into his chambers or bedroom? Maybe she just wanted to engage him in some ancient board game like Chess! I think what the Queen of Sheba wanted to do was to, in the recent vernacular of the streets, knock some boots! Now how many wives and concubines did Solomon have? The Bible says he had 700 wives and 300 concubines. He was obviously Mr. Playa Playa of his day!

God created the pleasures derived from sex, but for a righteous reason! But is it mathematically possible for every SINgle Christian to be married? Should there be a national lottery that determines who can get married and therefore have sexual relations with their spouse or if they lose, be forced to live a life of perpetual abstinence?

You may have noticed when I spelled SINgle, I spelled SIN in all capital letters. Yes, I did that on purpose as many married Christians feel that it is a SIN to be SINgle. That is the message espoused by the pastor of the church to which I belong. On the Sunday closest to Valentine's Day, the pastor, his wife, and all the married couples who wish to participate, line up in coordinated colored outfits and march into the sanctuary for the service. How are the SINgle Christians supposed to feel witnessing this spectacle? I paraphrase the words of Chevy Chase of "Saturday Night Live" fame when I think of this nonsensical act, "We are happily married and *you are not!*" I must add at this juncture that there are some SINgle Christians who have given up on ever being happy in a relationship. There are some Christian men and women who find the comfort of possessing material things more pleasurable and joyful in their lives than being in an unfulfilling relationship. I heard a former co-worker relate the following profound statement, "There is nothing worse than supposedly being in a committed relationship but feeling all alone!" I share this sentiment to the utmost and have chosen to be in a period of romantic and relationship retrenchment because I simply do not feel at this time that I have the requisite energy for another unfulfilling relationship! In addition, I accept full responsibility for all my failed relationships because I either jumped back into a new relationship too soon after a disastrous one or used an improper criteria for the women I pursued!

We all should get wiser as we age and mature, and Lord knows that I have made my mistakes just as you have. I have also blown some great opportunities to be in a blessed relationship because again, I was emotionally out of gas to pursue a relationship at the time a beautiful lady was ready to share her life with me!

What is the definition of insanity? Oh yes, insanity is doing the same thing over and over again expecting different results. But as my late mother used to say frequently, "Even IRON wears out!"

Let us look at what the Word of God says about being SINgle as it relates to premarital sex and fornication. I did mention from the outset that I would be discussing some controversial Biblical issues, right? Just checking!

1 Corinthians 6:18-20 New International Version (NIV) states, [18] Flee from sexual immorality. All other sins a person commits are outside the body, but whoever sins sexually, sins against their own body. [19] Do you not know that your bodies are temples of the Holy Spirit, who is in you, whom you have received from God? You are not your own; [20] you were bought at a price. Therefore honor God with your bodies.

There is a virtual plethora of similarly themed scriptures. You might also look at 1 Corinthians 7:2; where the Amplified Bible (AMP) reads

[2] But because of [the temptation to [participate in] sexual immorality, <u>let each man have his own wife</u>, and let

<u>each woman have her own husband.</u>

Hmm, but again that is achievable in today's society ... seriously?

In addition, you may also want to review Galatians 5:19-21; and 1 Corinthians 7 which is entitled in any Study Bible, Concerning Married Life.

The apostle Paul makes it perfectly clear that God frowns on premarital sex just as much as He does adultery, and let us be real, adultery is more pervasive than fast food restaurants in this country. Research published in well-respected media, such as the New York Times suggest that adultery is on the increase and frighteningly 33.3 % of married men cheat on their spouse while 25% of married women cheat on their spouse. The question now arises, with whom are they cheating? Let us also come to the realization that polygamy and polygyny (a man taking more than one wife or girlfriend) were a widespread practice in the era of the first century AD Christian church.

How do you know that, Brother James? I am glad you asked me that question as all we need do is look at the qualifications of a pastor and deacon located in I Timothy 3. In each instance, each man was to be the husband of ONE WIFE. So, we might assume correctly that polygamy and polygyny was ever-present in the first century AD. Hence, the necessity of this provision or qualification. Let me also state that a pastor or deacon need not be married. Paul never married, and neither did his protégé, Timothy, whom he gave these qualifications. Given that reality that a pastor and a deacon, if married, could ONLY have one wife, are polygamous relationships worthy of consideration today?

Do you know any people who cheat on their spouse?

I do, but I am not going to put them on blast, so no phone calls please, my married friends! My point is that some people are so greedy for the company or sex outside their marriage or simply feel unfulfilled in their relationship, they cheat, and this cheating may preclude some SINgle Christians from meeting their special someone. When people cheat, the person who is not married generally is devoted more to the cheating relationship, possibly missing the person God has intended for them. The Zen Buddhist suggests you will only meet your perfect match in life, that person with whom you could be evenly yoked, once every 28,000 years! And yes, I did not mistype the number 28,000 years!

    We live in an era where there are debates about legalizing drug use and prostitution. We have already borne witness to the legalization of gambling. The city of Detroit has three huge land-locked casinos, and there is one across the Detroit River in Windsor, Ontario, Canada. The question now arises, if God intends that every Christian should want to be married, why is there not a ready surplus of available and eligible Christians of the opposite sex from which to choose from? Should polygamy be legal? Please do not get me wrong. The perfect form of polygamy was to protect women, not to exploit them. So, I ask, if you are a SINgle woman desiring to be married, would you consent to be in a legal union as long as you were respected and all your needs were addressed? There are a lot of women of financial substance. Would you be willing to support multiple good husbands in this horrible economy as long as you were respected and protected? I love words, and two words that I love are "dejure," meaning by law and "defacto," meaning by tradition or custom. I respectfully suggest to you that while there are many dejure marriages in this country, there are many defacto polygamous relationships in this country, and if you do not believe me, just watch the Jerry Springer, Maury Povich, and Steve Wilkos shows as evidence of my assertion! Defacto polygamy is practiced under the cloak of darkness and secrecy, whether we approve of it or not! But the Bible says, what is done in the dark will come into the light.

So, how do we deal with the fact that people in this country are waiting later in life to get married? There are, according to the Census and Pew Reports, an increasing number of women who have never been married and who have a minimal, or more bluntly, a snowball's chance in Hell of ever being married. The number of women compared to the number of men in this country are not enormously greater. However, when one goes to a coed college campus, a nightclub, and even a more obvious scenario, church, the women outnumber the men at a ratio of at least 5 to 1. I submit to you that if you are a Christian woman looking for Mr. Right, the issue confronting you is not a question of available men. Rather, it is a question of eligible men! If we were to factor out of the equation of eligible men those who are incarcerated, perpetually unemployed, uneducated, those involved in an alternative lifestyle relationship, and those who subscribe to the lyrics of the song performed by Jerry Butler, I'm Giving Up On Love Before Love Gives Up On Me, the ratio of women to available eligible men is probably 10-1!

The divorce rate for first marriages is at 50%, while the divorce rate for second marriages is roughly 67%, and the divorce rate for third marriages is approximately 74%. With these startling statistics, how could one be expected to abstain from sexual relations if they are not married and love the Lord?

We all know someone who goes to church regularly, but is engaged in some type of physical, uncommitted relationship. I think this is what is commonly referred to as, friends with benefits. I am not trying to get in your business, but are you abstaining from sexual relations as a SINgle Christian? Do you feel because you are an active church member, the Lord will look the other way when you address that sexual desire, or as we said in my youth, that itch I cannot scratch! If you have found a righteous way to address this plague of sexual desires, please tell us how to be true to the Word of God and be a SINgle, Saved, and Satisfied Christian who abstains from premarital sex. I am addressing both my SINgle sisters and brothers in Christ. A basic short prayer that is apropos here is, help me/us Jesus!

Honestly, I do not have an answer for our dilemma, but as the lyrics of a Donnie McClurkin song comes to mind, "We fall down, but we get up!" Donnie McClurkin suggests that we repent; however, true repentance means we turn away from our sins and stop committing then repenting the same sin over and over again! Whew! Is all this Christian talk about obeying God's Word regarding abstinence bothering and confusing you? Excuse me while I take a long, cold shower because the image of a very attractive lady I admittedly lust after just popped into my mind. I will be back in an hour. Okay, I am back.

I think I have already mentioned that I am a Preacher's Kid (PK), but that truth should not imply I am always righteous and have all the answers. I ask again, is God fair in all He does because when I am alone, I might ask God, why me Lord? Why me? How could God justify subjecting millions of Christian SINgles to a life of not being in a meaningful relationship? How could the Lord say that many SINgle Christians should never be in a monogamous common law relationship where the parties are truly committed to one another, spiritually, intellectually, financially, emotionally, and sexually? Some make the argument that Adam and Eve,

Boaz and Ruth, and Isaac and Rebekah were never "legally" married, but we must use hermeneutics (the science of proper interpretation, especially of scriptures) to understand God's Divine and ultimate plan for us.

Have you prayed for that special mate to appear in your life to no avail? Are you using a God-centered criteria for your mate, or do you reject a potential God-given mate because they do not look like a movie star? I love a profound statement my son, Hamadi, made as we discussed this issue. Dad, I do not need a ten, I just need a seven, as long as she is willing to work with me to achieve mutual goals!

An effective planner always has a Plan A and Plan B. What, my friend, is your Plan B to deal with the pain of being alone, possibly for the remainder of your life? Can you be like Willona on Good Times who was questioned about not having a man and stated, "I may be alone, but I'm not lonely!" Can you truthfully subscribe to Willona's posture about being SINgle?

Given the startling statistics regarding unmarried Christian folks in this land, is there a need for a proclamation from the pulpits that every SINgle Christian needs to take three lengthy COLD showers every day?

Again, I do not have the answer, but I know too many folks who are tired of being alone, of not being in a committed and loving relationship. They are tired of going home to an empty place unless they have pets. They are exhaustingly tired of getting dressed for work and church but not out for the evening with someone whom with they are evenly yoked!

I have a spiritual praise ritual I exercise each and every morning. When I first awaken, I say, thank you, Lord, for allowing me to see a new day. I then get out of bed, get my

Bible that I keep in my bedroom, and then I pray. I start each prayer thanking God for all He has done, is doing, and will do in my life and the lives of my loved ones. Recognizing that I have two SINgle sisters, a multitude of SINgle female cousins, and numerous SINgle female and male friends, I ask the Lord to bless them with the special person they long for, that special person of their dreams. I then name all the people I know that I would want the Lord to bless with the desires of their hearts as long as their desires do not come into direct conflict with God's Divine Will for them. I especially pray that He blesses each person named with that very special someone.

    I read a psychology book many years ago where the thesis is no SANE person wants to be alone. I know that I do not always enjoy being alone, but sometimes I sincerely appreciate my solitude.

    If you are alone, but are engaged in a "friends with benefits" relationship, earnestly pray for forgiveness, asking God to direct you to that place where you may meet your special someone. I, for one, cannot and will not condemn you for exercising your natural physical desires the Lord placed within you, but be careful because the Lord is ALWAYS watching!

    Please do not run and tell your pastor, I am encouraging you to SIN by being in a common law relationship or that I condone your having premarital relationships as I have. Simply tell your pastor to pray for me as I pray for you. Moreover, please know that should you fall down on the issues discussed, I will never, ever judge you, and I do truly understand your desire to love and have your love reciprocated!

ARTICLE 19

Does Your Pastor Meet The Biblical Criteria Of an Effective Church Leader?

Let us be very honest! The contemporary church is in serious trouble, very serious trouble. Most of the churches across this country are experiencing financial difficulties. Revenue, or should I say, tithes and offerings appear to be on an irreversible downward spiral. This fact has led to the phenomena of churches going into foreclosure at an alarming rate of eleven churches per month! Please, if you do not believe me, please google, "churches in foreclosure, "and you will see over 34 million hits on this topic. I say again, the Houses of Worship are in serious trouble.

There are many churches whose previous attendance required two or three services on Sundays to accommodate their membership. Now, many of these churches have reverted to only one service on Sunday. And when we couple this fact with the trend that the millennials are not regularly attending church, or contributing to the houses of God, the new reality portends an ominous message about the future of the Christian church.

So, what can be done to turn this negative situation around? Well, my simple answer is that the truth of God's Word must be taught across the pulpits, and the character of the pastor of each and every church must be above reproach. The Bible clearly teaches that a pastor's conduct be "blameless". Blameless does not mean that people cannot find and share any personal dirt on the pastor because we all have been lied on and disparaged, and pastors are no exception to that reality. Please allow me to illustrate my point of having one's character castigated via the lyrics of the James Cleveland song, "As Long As I Got King Jesus."

I've Been Lied On (lied on) Cheated (cheated) Talked About (talked about) Mistreated (mistreated) I've been abused (abused) Scorned (scorned) Talked about sure as you're born (talked about sure as you're born) I've been up (up) Down (down) Almost To the Ground (almost to the ground) Long as I got King Jesus (long as I got King Jesus) Long, Long, Long, as I got him I don't need nobody else!

So, blameless in the Biblical context does not mean that a person's character cannot be challenged. No, blameless in the Biblical sense means that malicious lies, rumors, and denigrating attacks on a Christian, especially a pastor should never be found to be true!

So, it is imperative that we look at the qualifications of a church leader (pastor, elder, apostle, bishop, etc. or whatever title your church leader uses) so we will know with a great deal of clarity and certainty if he or she is living a life that aids in the restoration of the Christian church.

My late father, Reverend Robert W. James, often said, "Jesus was the model preacher." My Father was also a great admirer of the epistles/letters written by the apostle Paul. In another Article, I mentioned Paul's noteworthy espousal that he would rather DIE than receive a salary from those whom he preached the gospel of Jesus Christ. Paul chose to work as a tentmaker to earn his living so he might not be a financial burden on the churches he established. Oh, I love my mother's absolute favorite scripture where Paul speaks of being content with the provisions of God as he worked unselfishly in the Lord's vineyard. In his epistle to the church in Philippi, Paul wrote, "[10] I rejoiced greatly in the Lord that at last you renewed your concern for me. Indeed, you were concerned, but you had no opportunity to show it. [11] I am not saying this because I am in need, for I have learned to be content whatever the circumstances. [12] I know what it is to be in need, and I know what it is to have plenty. I have learned the secret of being content in any and every situation, whether well fed or hungry, whether living in plenty or in want. [13] I can do all this through him who gives me strength. (Philippian's 4:10-13, NIV)."

I certainly do not imply that the pastors of today should not be allowed to earn a living from preaching the Gospel. Rather, I am saying that those pastors who, like Jesus, the Disciples, and Paul, preached the Gospel for FREE because it was given to them freely, are to be commended. How can a pastor exhort you to sacrifice financially, insisting you give "until it hurts," while they drive a Bentley and live in a mansion on a hill? So, please allow me to do a Shout Out to those men and women of God who do not charge their congregations exorbitant salaries! I know two such men in Detroit who live off their retirement incomes, Pastor Joseph Chatten and Pastor Jake Gaines. Gentlemen, I sincerely applaud you for what you do for the Lord, FREELY!

Our best starting point to ascertain whether or not your pastor is an effective church leader is to look at the list of qualifications, or should I say, the job description that the apostle Paul presented to his protégé, Timothy, in his epistle, I Timothy 3:1-7. Let us carefully look at these qualifications so we may discern if the person residing in the pulpit at your church is the cause for the decline in church attendance. Maybe some of the people who have left your church have joined another church. There are people who jump from one congregation to another once they discover they cannot be a ministry head, or they simply do not like the pastor. My late mother referred to these folks as "Gypsy" Christians. Do you know any Gypsy Christians? Are you prone to leave a church because of dissatisfaction with a particular ministry, ministry leader, or the pastor? Or, are you upset simply with what goes on there? Hmm, are you a Gypsy Christian? Are you contributing to the decline in attendance at several churches in your community?

Now let us look at I Timothy 3:1-7. What follows in bold type is the word of God, and what follows in parenthesis is my comments related to the criteria of a pastor. The NIV translation of I Timothy 3:1-7 reads thusly, Whoever aspires to be an overseer desires a noble task.

[2] Now the overseer is to be above reproach, (*above reproach means that a pastor cannot be discredited for any reason! Does your pastor always exercise due diligence in the performance of his duties? I know a pastor who cancelled Home Going services on Saturdays saying they interfered with his ministry. The truth is he loves to play golf and has a boat he cruises and parties on during the summer. Therefore, conducting God's work on Saturdays is a major inconvenience to his life of leisure and is not an obstacle to his ministry! I think it callous to remove Saturdays as an option for bereaved families because some folks have family out of town who now have to take more days off to attend a funeral of a loved one conducted Monday through Friday. What an inconvenience to the families! What an egregious failure to carry out his duties as a pastor!*) **faithful to his wife,** (*I am reminded of the scandals related to Jim Bakker, Jimmy Swaggart, Zachery Tims, Eddie Long, Ted Haggard, Benny Hinn, and countless other unfaithful men of the cloth. I have been told numerous*

stories by credible people regarding pastors' numerous infidelities. All the while these cheaters pretend to be ultra-pious. However, the Word of God says in Luke 8:17 (NIV) *For there is nothing hidden that will not be disclosed, and nothing concealed that will not be known or brought out into the open.* We all have something to hide, right? There are no perfect people, correct? So, what do you think your pastor is concealing and one day will be brought into the light if he/she was not called by the Lord to preach?). Temperate, self-controlled, respectable, (*There is a pastor in my city who one Sunday became distraught and agitated because he thought he should be receiving incessant amen's, that he shouted to the ushers to open the doors at the rear of the sanctuary so everyone who was not giving him his desired amens might leave and go to another church! That was just one of the many aberrant and unwarranted outbursts obviously from this so-called man of God!*) hospitable, (*Are there cliques in your church? Does everyone get equal attention from your pastor? Do you feel as if you have to kiss his ring or that part of his/her anatomy where the sun does not shine to meet with his/her Excellency about a personal issue? Well, depending on your answers, I respectfully suggest to you your pastor is inhospitable rather than hospitable in the eyes of some fellow congregants, and more importantly, in the eyes of the Lord!*) able to teach, (*Oh Lord, here is where I lose it! There is so much garbage emanating from too many pulpits that I know that there are two views on being able to teach. There are some pastors who do excellent research and are adroit at distorting God's Word. Their congregants fall in lock step and would allow this Judas goat to lead them directly to Hell. Do you remember Jim Jones? The other gifted teachers use the principles of hermeneutics and teach their congregants the truth of God's Word. I believe the latter group of pastors is in a distinct minority.*) [3] not given to drunkenness, (*the Word of*

God has no prohibitions about drinking alcohol, but, how can men or women of God perform their duties as a shepherd if they cannot control their intake of alcohol? Let us contemplate on that for a minute.) not violent but gentle, (*I do not want to sound like I am pastor-bashing, but I witnessed a pastor start an argument with another congregant because the pastor was supposed to speak at another church on a weeknight when a ministry meeting was also being held. The pastor loudly and rudely admonished this congregant in front of his wife and numerous others in an ungodly way. I had to position myself between them before any punches were thrown. This same pastor also was alleged (wink, wink) to have physically abused his wife in the early years of his ministry. He, the pastor, went to jail and would be keenly surprised to know who just might have a copy of the incident report from that fateful night of wife beating!*) not quarrelsome, (*I need not expound on this issue, given my previous statements above*) not a lover of money. (*If you have not captured the essence of my major complaint against some pastors, this is it! If God called men and women to preach, why do they not do it for a respectable wage like a person who works for one of the Big 3 in Detroit? Why must a pastor become wealthy from preaching the Gospel, and, in many instances a false gospel such as the prosperity gospel? All I can say is, Help Me Jesus!*) [4] He must manage his own family well and see that his children obey him, and he must do so in a manner worthy of full respect. [[5] If anyone does not know how to manage his own family, how can he take care of God's church?] (*There is an old saying, "Preachers have the worst kids!" That is not always true. However, in those instances where PK's do get in trouble, I believe it is due to one of two factors. First, PK's are held to such a higher standard of conduct that we might act out just so we might fit in with the most notable social set. Or, PK's get into trouble because of what they see at home from* their parents. If PK's see drinking, adultery, cursing, back biting, etc. in their living room, how can one expect them not to emulate their parents? Many of the people I have known who spent time behind bars had role models in their parents. Enough said?) ⁶ He must not be a recent convert, or he may become conceited and fall under the same judgment as the devil. (*This dictum was necessary in the early days of the Christian church and should be carefully considered in this era where young people should be allowed to preach if that is their true calling! Christianity is not NEW today!*) ⁷ He must also have a good reputation with outsiders, so that he will not fall into disgrace and into the devil's trap. (*I am aware of a church where the pastor has an extremely bad reputation! Why? Because this egomaniacal man will not let anyone who has accepted the calling to preach, to preach in HIS pulpit! Let me give you an example. This church usually has two services on Sundays, but this pastor wants to do other things on Sunday mornings in the summer, so he called for a vote to go to one service on Sundays in the summer. There was an ill-attended meeting at this church to put the number of services to a vote. The pastor won by a slim margin. But, if he wants his Sunday mornings off, oh, by the way, what is the earliest tee time one can get ... on a Sunday morning? I am sorry, I digressed. So, if this pastor has ten or more ministers in his pulpit, why not continue to have two services in the summer and give the ministers in his pulpit an opportunity to preach? This pastor in my mind is the poster child for the Most Undeserving Of Respect Pimp In The Pulpit Award. This slimy degenerate is the type of person about which Paul warned Timothy.*)

Politely, could your pastor pass ALL the qualifications of being an outstanding church leader? The Word of God informs us that if we were to break one Biblical command, we have in essence broken them ALL! With that premise in mind, again, I ask, could your pastor pass all the tenets or qualifications of a religious leader? We might want to use a pass/fail scoring system, but how does Almighty God grade your pastor or my pastor? Let me assure you there is only a pass/fail grading system in God's eyes, and the question now arises, how many pastors truly meet the well-defined and narrow qualifications of an elder, bishop, pastor, apostle, etc.?

Okay, let us put my theory to the test. I will provide you with a seven question test that will determine if your pastor is an effective and respected leader in your community. Given the size of your church and community:

1. Is your pastor asked to speak at revivals and other special church programs at least 12 times per year? Yes [ ] No [ ]
2. When pastor vacancies are announced in your community, are any of the associate ministers trained by your pastor given consideration? Yes [ ] No [ ]
3. Is your pastor an active participant in a nursing home or jail ministry? Yes [ ] No [ ]
4. Can you call your pastor early in the morning/AM and expect to have him/her immediately address your needs/situations? Yes [ ] No [ ]
5. Is your pastor an active member in the governing body of your denomination on the local/ or national level? IE, National Baptist Convention. Yes [ ] No [ ]
6. At special anniversary programs at your church, does your pastor have a varied number of guest speakers participating each year, or does he/she use the same people over and over again? Yes [ ] No [ ]
7. Is your pastor a highly regarded teacher of God's Word in your community? Yes [ ] No [ ]

Please grade your own test and tell yourself and others if your pastor is an effective leader of God's people in your community!

I believe, as I have indicated before in this and other Articles, the Pareto Principle is in full effect. Twenty percent of pastors truly work giving their all in God's best interest while 80% reap the benefits. Serious across the board changes are required to stem the tide of decline in church attendance and financial support witnessed today. Some of the aforementioned church decline is due to the aberrant economy, but most are due to the failure of greedy pastors who only want to become wealthy off God's Word! I could be wrong, but I do not think so! Serious changes are needed in God's houses of worship, and taking in the words from the lyrics of a Sam Cooke song, "A change is gonna come!"

ARTICLE 20

Do You Aspire To Be A Church Celebrity?

May I ask you a few questions? If your church attendance is regular, are you able on Mondays to inform someone about the title of the sermon and the content of its message? Can you also share with someone the songs rendered by your choir and how both the sermon and the music made you feel ready for the world on Monday? Can you name the people in your church who have the finest automobiles and provide someone with the year of production, make and model of same? Could you make a list of all the finest dressed congregants in your house of worship, describing the fashion designer names of their attire, including their shoes? Do you qualify as being one of the best dressed members of your House of Worship? Can you name the leaders of the various church ministries that are indubitably qualified to hold their respective position? Are there cliques based upon titles and the attendant associations with certain ministries in your Church?

Well, if you cannot answer yes to the first two questions but can answer the majority of the other questions, maybe, just maybe, you aspire to be a church celebrity or, you know someone who wants to be one.

So, Brother James, what is your real point here? What are you really saying about people in church these days?

My late mother, a pastor's wife, often said, "Some

people come to church to be filled with the Holy Ghost while others just want to be seen in their fine and expensive attire. They just want to be church celebrities!"

Unfortunately, there are those whose primary reason for attending church is not to worship. For some, worship has been relegated to a tertiary position of consideration because they opt to be worshipped!

There have been people I have encountered throughout my Christian life who are so arrogant, pompous, and egomaniacal that upon seeing them I want to regurgitate my breakfast. These folks dress fine, live in fine homes, and carry themselves as if everyone else in the environment reeks of a pungent odor. In actuality, it is not the rest of us who stink, it is the ever-present pungent odor of these folk's stinky, superior attitudes! Not hating on anyone, just telling the truth! Come on, if you were to make a list of such people, how many names would appear?

Please do not get upset with me for telling the truth! I have friends all across this country who are devout Christians, but who worship in the isolation of their homes because they do not feel compelled to bow down to a Church Celebrity or Church Celebrities! Oh, I love the words of Carter G. Woodson, the founder of Black History Month and author of, *"The Mis-Education of the Negro,"* when he suggested that too many African Americans, upon getting a degree, laud their education over their less educated neighbors, even though they have menial jobs or jobs not commensurate to their achieved level of education. Do you know people in your church that have a haughty attitude toward you and act as if they have a special relationship with the Lord that you need to "recognize"?

My good friend and mentor, Pastor Jake Gaines,

Pastor of Synagogue Baptist Church in Detroit, Michigan, related to a class I was in that there are some folks who come to church to seek a title. This gifted pastor treats his congregants with as much equality, as is humanly possible. And, if you are a Christian man who attends his church on Communion Sunday, be prepared to stand up with the deacons as Holy Communion is served. His message to me is that the deacons are equal to me and others as we are ALL servants to Christ.

I appreciate the sentiment expressed by Richard Pryor, who said something like, "I am happy for anyone with money and status as long as they came by it honestly." I do, however, reserve the right to express my disdain for people who think that because God has blessed them, that they are superior to others! As a PK I have seen this miscreant attitude manifest itself in many Houses of Worship. What did Jesus do? Did He bless the rich, or did He bless the poor? Did Jesus hang out with the rich and famous celebrities of His day, or did He associate with the downtrodden, the under-employed, hard-working people of meager socio-economic circumstances? Please take a minute to think about my questions. Go ahead, I have time!

Another good friend of mine in the ministry, Pastor Joseph Chatten, Pastor of Resurrection Mission Baptist Church in Berkley, Michigan, shares this position of equality of people in God's House. Whenever he is invited to churches for events, he is asked, by virtue of his pastoral status, to sit on the dais or at a table with other pastors. Rather than seek the "elevated" position of status, he opts to sit at the table with his wife and congregants. This is an expression of God's contempt for those who seek a superior status in his Houses of Worship.

This is a perfect juncture to interject some scripture

into my posture concerning church celebrities!

The NIV translation of James 2:1-4 reads thusly, "[1] My brothers and sisters, believers in our glorious Lord Jesus Christ must not show favoritism. [2] Suppose a man comes into your meeting wearing a gold ring and fine clothes, and a poor man in filthy old clothes also comes in. [3] If you show special attention to the man wearing fine clothes and say, "Here's a good seat for you," but say to the poor man, "You stand there" or "Sit on the floor by my feet," [4] have you not discriminated among yourselves and become judges with evil thoughts?"

About a decade ago, the church where my membership exists conducted a unique exercise on the treatment of strangers in the church. There was a session during Vacation Bible School, where a man reeking of alcohol, a woman dressed as a prostitute, and a man who had all the trappings of a homeless person entered the sanctuary and sat in the midst of the "Christians" in the sanctuary. The "good" Christians were so repulsed by these perceived destitute interlopers that they expeditiously removed themselves from the presence of these distressed individuals. Just before the session concluded, it was revealed that the alleged drunk, a prostitute, and homeless man were just fellow congregants in disguise. This was an excellent exercise that exposed how we might talk a good game about being like Jesus, but when the proverbial human waste material hits the fan, people, will operate in their real comfort level. It was obvious that many of the assembled congregants, or should I say, good Christians deported themselves in a very un-Christ like manner. These folks relegated those whom they found to be inferior to seats at their feet!

How do you treat visitors to your church? Do you welcome them as Jesus would, and do you check out their attire or find out who invited them?

Just in case you know someone who either has a title and lauds their title over you or you know someone in your church who is jockeying for a position, a title, you just might know a wannabe church celebrity!

The reason I am sharing this position is that I believe in every church of a decent size, there are congregants who only come to be a Church Celebrity. Do you have people who spend a small fortune to be on the best dressed list for a church anniversary, pastor's anniversary, Men's and Women's Day? The church where I am a member has a mannequin, yes, a mannequin, in the vestibule of the church with the uniform of the day for Men's Day. The outfits have a certain shirt, pants, and sports jacket so that the men of this church are "uniform in their attire." I opt out of this nonsensical posture. I can afford to spend a couple of hundred dollars for a one day uniform, but would my money be better served if I and the other men made a donation to a Soup Kitchen or Homeless Shelter? The brothers have STOPPED asking me to purchase a Men's Day uniform as I have shared a sentiment I learned from Kwame Toure, formerly known as Stokely Carmichael, "We do not always have to be uniform to be unified!"

There is another scripture that is apropos at this point in my discourse. The scripture located at Galatians 3:28-29 in the NIV translations clearly shows us there are NO church celebrities. This scripture eloquently reads, "[26] so in Christ Jesus you are all children of God through faith, [27] for all of you who were baptized into Christ have clothed yourselves with Christ. [28] There is neither Jew nor Gentile, neither slave nor free, nor is there male and female, for you are all one in Christ Jesus. [29] If you belong to Christ, then you are Abraham's seed, and heirs according to the promise." Wow, maybe those who feel the rest of us should bow down to them need to read this enlightening scripture and govern themselves accordingly!

I sincerely pray that I have made my point that there is absolutely no room for this type of conduct and egoism of anyone in the sanctuaries of God. Never let yourself fall into the social trap of following the crowd or leaders whose actions and words are not in line with the teachings of Jesus Christ. Please do not put anyone on a pedestal in your church, not even your elder, pastor, apostle, etc. I recently saw instances on the reality TV shows, Pastors of ..., where the pastor entered into a conference room and everyone waiting for their religious leader leaped to their feet. I concluded their conduct was in honor and reverence to their religious leader. Show me the scripture where the disciples or anyone else jumped to a standing position when Jesus entered a room where people were assembled and waiting for Him. Again, I respectfully ask that you show me the scripture that even remotely suggests such a reverential posture.

Please do not feel inferior to ANYONE in your church, and please do not follow any scripturally based actions without question.

If you follow someone, do not follow a church celebrity, follow the wisest people in your midst. I love what Alexander the Great said on whom to follow in life, "I do not fear an army of lions led by a lamb. I do fear an army of sheep led by a lion."

The Word of God is crystal clear on the issue whom we should revere in our lives within and without God's sanctuaries. Acts 5:29 of the NIV translation of the Bible illuminates my posture as it states, "29 Peter and the other apostles replied: 'We must obey God rather than human beings!" So, I pray you are not offended by what I have expressed in this discourse. After all, why would we try to be worshipped or follow those who aspire to be church celebrities when the Word of God found at Acts 10:34 succinctly and clearly states, "Then Peter opened *his* mouth, and said, of a truth I perceive that God is no RESPECTER of PERSONS!!!"

ARTICLE 21

Do You TRULY Understand What You Are Doing When You Say, . . . "AMEN"?

Believers and nonbelievers alike have more than likely used the word "amen" after hearing another person speak on some topic. The word "amen" is always used on Sundays as deacons, ministry leaders, Sunday School teachers, and pastors invoke the congregation to "cosign" and commit to some point they/the speaker just made. But, do we truly realize what we are saying when we say, "AMEN"?

The Nelson's New Illustrated Bible Dictionary defines the word "amen" thusly, "a solemn word by which a person confirms a statement, an oath, or a covenant. It is also used in worship to affirm an address, psalm, or prayer." In essence, when we say "amen," we are saying we are in complete and total agreement with the speaker who says in the form of a question, "amen"? Also, when a sermon is not eliciting the desired response, a very emotional response from the religious leaders presentation he/she might say, "everybody ought to be saying "amen" right about now." Or, they may say, "Can I get an "AMEN"?" And many people will say "amen" so the dry and exceedingly boring sermon may come to an expeditious end. Or, they might be caught in the momentary religious fervor and say "amen" because everyone else is saying "amen." Come on now, I am not the only person who was bored to tears by a sermon and the pastor was relentlessly pandering for an "amen," so we simply said

"AMEN"! We gave in to the pastor as we looked at our watch and thought to ourselves, I sure hope he/she wraps up this sermon because I have things to do!

But were we in complete and total agreement with the speaker? Many times I think not! So, when the pastor is talking about tithing, and we do not tithe but say "AMEN," whom are we fooling? Certainly not God. When the sermon is about not fornicating or committing adultery and we commit one of these sins, yet we say "amen," what are we doing?

Are we not putting our salvation in question if we say we agree but do not repent of our sins? After all, we did say at the urging of the pastor, "AMEN." Worse yet, is when a pastor is preaching on the prosperity, name it, and claim it, and my most hated false gospel, then you must plant a monetary seed to gain favor with God, and then say "AMEN" to this garbage espoused by the pastor. Do we truly understand and realize what we are doing? The Apostle Paul made it emphatically and abundantly clear in the first chapter of Galatians that there is only one true gospel, the gospel of Jesus Christ. So, why do we subscribe to these impure, distorted, and false doctrines, giving our pastor an ardent "AMEN" as they cajole us to place an exaggerated emphasis on money and the acquisition of material possessions as opposed to focusing on the Lord? We gladly and with great fervor say "AMEN"! Are we not sinning in the eyes of the Lord?

I remember as a very young baptized child that when I attended the neighborhood church and we were asked to read the Baptist Church Covenant, the pastor would emphatically inform us not to read aloud any portion of the Covenant to which we did not agree. In essence, he instructed us not to commit to any of the provisions of the covenant we knew we were going to break, like abstaining from alcohol, if we knew we were going to knock back a couple of cool ones after church. Please remember, I was a child, but I remember to this day the import of not lying to the Lord in church. To read the entire Church Covenant aloud, knowing that I did not agree with some of its precepts, was akin to saying "Amen!" Is not lying, especially in church, a sin? That posture has stayed with me forever, and it spawned my desire to write this particular article. This preacher was saying, "Do not say "AMEN" if you do not agree with any of the covenant provisions!"

I am reminded at this juncture of the story of Ananias and Sapphira, in Acts 4:32 - 5:1-11. What must be understood is that in the first century AD church, some of the Christian believers agreed to sell their property to support the church. Has your church ever had a building fund to which you gave generously? But, I digress. Let us get back to the story. Peter was collecting funds to build a church and asked the believers to sell their property and give all the money to the church. Ananias and his wife Sapphira sold their property, but withheld a portion of the proceeds for themselves, which was contrary to the agreement they had willingly made. Remember, all the believers were in complete and total agreement and had in essence said "AMEN" to Peter's request to sell their property and give ALL the proceeds to the church. When Peter confronted Ananias, he lied and said he and his wife gave all the money, and his wife Sapphira had handed over the entire proceeds from the sale of their land. Peter told Ananias, **"You have not lied just to human beings, but to God."** Ananias dropped dead and was immediately taken out and buried. Three hours later, Sapphira, unaware of what had happened, was asked by Peter if she and her husband gave him all the money from the sale of their property. She responded, "Yes," and then Peter told her that the young men entering the room had just buried her husband for his sin of lying, and she too dropped dead!

Is God Fair

While neither Ananias nor his wife, Sapphira, are recorded to have said "AMEN" to Peter's request to sell their property, they were in complete and total agreement with the plan and might as well have said "AMEN."

So, let us be wary of saying "amen" on all occasions just so others may think we are in agreement with them or the pastor when in actuality we are not! The next time someone cajoles you to say "AMEN," meaning you are in agreement, think before you speak, and reflect upon the story of Ananias and his wife, Sapphira!

You might fool some of the people some of the time, but you will never fool God at any time!

ARTICLE 22

Are You A SUCKA For A PIMP In The Pulpit?

SUCKA: One who is easily deceived or cheated; a dupe (an idiot or fool).

I know, here I go again! Yes, I am a PK, a preacher's kid, so why do I use the language of the streets in this book as often as I do? I do it to get your attention! I do not want to see anyone anywhere being abused, and I contend that there is an egregious amount of abuse disguised as good Bible teaching being heaped upon God's people by those who claim to be the guardians, the shepherds of God's people.

When I think about the dedication, the suffering, the ultimate sacrifices, and the meager lifestyles of Jesus, His Disciples, and the Apostle Paul compared to many preachers today, I am truly dismayed. Yes, Paul said that a preacher of the gospel had the right to be paid for his services, but did Paul suggest that the preachers of the gospel be paid so well that they may live far away from their congregations in luxurious mansions? Did Paul suggest that preachers live so well that their congregants cannot afford to drive to, let alone live in the same neighborhoods? Did Paul or Jesus remotely suggest that today's preachers should drive their pimp-mobile, I mean their Rolls Royce, Bentley, Mercedes Benz, or BMW's around town, ignoring the escalating crime, neighborhood blight, rampant alcohol, hard drug substance abuse, and other social ills adversely impacting their community? No, Jesus, Paul, and the Disciples lived a life serving the Almighty God, and their lives were absent of the luxurious lifestyles we witness today in the phenomena of the megachurch and televised ministries.

A few years back, I was facilitating a Bible Study, and the subject of the luxurious lifestyles of certain preachers in Detroit arose. Many of the attendees thought it shameful how these preachers were living in the grandest suburbs and driving automobiles that cost more than the residences of many of the folks in the Bible Study. Not surprisingly, however, one participant spoke up in defense of these pimps in the pulpit and said people want their pastor to be better situated than they because, "Jesus wasn't poor!" I thought to myself, "What Bible does this individual read?" How could anyone read the Synoptic Gospels or any other books of the New Testament and come to such a distorted conclusion that Jesus Christ, Jesus of Nazareth, and Jesus the Son of God, was not poor!

I then thought, I bet there have been sermons at this individual's church about the various forms of the prosperity gospel and the pastor led this person and countless others to believe it was okay for him to wear fine clothes, send his children to private schools, vacation on the European continent, eat in the finest 5-star restaurants, and drive a Bentley while his wife and children all drove expensive automobiles because he was like Jesus and Jesus was not POOR! I bet this person's pastor never preached on the qualifications of being an elder, bishop, etc. in I Timothy 3, and if he did, he must have glossed over the dictate of NOT preaching for filthy lucre. Or, possibly the person I am alluding to did not understand that lucre was just another word for M-O-N-E-Y!

So, I started this article disparaging this mindset ever-present in this country where people are making their religious leader a little "g" god and are inadvertently looking at some man or woman as their lord and savior. I respectfully suggest to you, if you are constantly heard saying, "Well, my pastor said, or My pastor drives a, or My pastor lives in," instead of saying confidently, "The Word of God says," then chances are you are a *Sucka For A pimp in the pulpit*!

I am an avid viewer of Real Time with Bill Maher on HBO. Bill Maher delights in poking fun at people of any religious beliefs, especially Christians. He revels in the fact promoted by the Pew Report that Christianity is on what appears to be an irreversible decline. He frequently refers to God's Word as nonsense and Jewish Fairy Tales. If I were to meet Mr. Maher, I would politely suggest to him there is absolute truth in God's Word, but the decline in people professing to being Christians is not due to the Word of God but to the distorted way it is being taught. I would suggest that all he need do is sit back and watch this decline escalate because the generation of the millennials has lost faith, not in God, but in those who distort the Word of God for personal and financial gain. The Baby Boomers and the generations up to the millennials will die off, and the brick and mortar churches will slowly go the way of Borders Books, Circuit City etc. However, God WILL present a way to bring the millennials and the generations that follow them back into the fold! There are no trends or situations which God cannot reverse. However, people will stop going to church in mass in the next 20 years due to the distorted teachings being espoused by too many preachers today! I have heard too many Christians say that they can no longer <u>afford</u> to go to church because all the pastor does is beg for money!

There are too many distortions of God's Word for me to address in this article of my book; however, I do have three pet peeves that I will expound upon! My three pet peeves of distorted teachings of the word of God are: God does not give us the spirit of fear, tithing, and you need to plant a monetary seed to be blessed by the Lord.

I once dated a beautiful and intelligent woman whose belief in God was unquestionable. She worked late hours and would drop by my house for a few hours after work. We would often have stimulating conversations about current events and religion. On one such evening she was a little stressed from the job and told me she was going to stop by the neighborhood party store (in DC these stores are called Mom & Pop stores) to pick up a bottle of wine. I am not trying to say anything disparaging about Detroit, but I suggested that I give her a bottle of wine so she would not have to stop in an unsavory neighborhood to make her late night purchase. She politely said her pastor said, "God does not give us the spirit of fear!" I immediately responded, "but He does give us discernment, so please allow me to give you a bottle of wine." I remember that conversation as if it occurred yesterday because I hear it so much and so often.

There was a well-publicized carjacking of a prominent Detroit pastor, who was allegedly driving an $80k vehicle, dressed in an expensive designer outfit that matched the color of his automobile of which there were only four of this make and model in the entire state of Michigan, and was wearing a $40k watch! The problem was he was in an unsavory neighborhood known for its inordinately high crime rate, especially robberies, prostitution, and drug dealing when he was mugged. The rumor that permeated the city was, when asked by his congregation and the media as to why of all the gas stations he could have gotten his gas from at such an ungodly hour, why did he stop at this particular out of his way gas station. Again, rumor has it that he immediately retorted, "God does not give us the spirit of fear!" Hmm, I guess that is his story, and he is sticking to it! But is that what Paul was suggesting to his protégé Timothy, when he made that declaration? Since God does not give us the spirit of fear, does that mean I could walk through any well-known crime riddled neighborhood with Floyd Mayweather's thick stacks of money and not be fearful of being mugged, if not murdered? I know that the Lord is my protector, but come on ladies and gentlemen; God does give us common sense, which is coupled with a healthy dose of appropriate and appreciable fear! Does the Holy Spirit not tell us to listen to him in certain questionable situations?

I know that the Word of God gives us many examples where God's devoted servants were in fear for their lives! However, before we go there, let us look at just what Paul actually meant when he told Timothy that God does not give us the spirit of fear. All we need to do is to contrast the King James Version (KJV) of II Timothy 1:7 to the same verse in the NIV where we would find the following. [7] For God hath not given us the spirit of fear; but of power, and of love, and of a sound mind (KJV). But what we need to do is a Greek to English word study of the word fear in this verse in the KJV to discover the true and intended context of the author, Paul. To accomplish this word study, we might consult a Strong's Exhaustive Concordance of the Bible. We would then look in alphabetic order for the word fear, then locate the specific scripture reference. Once that act is accomplished, we would look for the 4-digit number associated with the word fear in the Greek portion of the Concordance, and therein we will find the exact meaning of Paul's word fear and its proper context.

Now let us look at the NIV translation of this scripture so we might have even greater clarity of Paul's meaning. Let

Is God Fair

us look at II Timothy 1:6-8. [6] For this reason I remind you to fan into flame the gift of God, which is in you through the laying on of my hands. [7] For the Spirit God gave us does not make us timid, but gives us power, love and self-discipline. [8] So do not be ashamed of the testimony about our Lord or of me his prisoner. Rather, join with me in suffering for the gospel, by the power of God (NIV).

Wow, Paul was telling Timothy to not be TIMID. In other words, he should be demonstratively aggressive when it came to preaching the gospel. In the current vernacular of the streets, Paul was suggesting that Timothy MAN UP and be self-confident! Why? Timothy was the first elder/bishop in the city of Ephesus, and he was in his mid-30s. In the first century AD, for people to have respect in their respective community, they were expected to be at least 40 years of age, which was the average lifespan of that epoch. Paul knew that Timothy would face many doctrinal challenges from the older male members of the church in Ephesus. Paul was saying not to let anyone intimidate him, since he was both a stranger and younger than the men in this new church. Paul also told Timothy to be bold because he was strong in his knowledge of the gospel.

Think about this, when a well-established pastor dies, retires, or leaves for a larger congregation, there is a search for a new pastor. The leaders of the church will accept the applications of several applicants who want to have their own congregation. Let us suppose a youthful and gifted minister with tremendous potential becomes pastor. Given the youth of the new pastor coupled with his perceived inexperience, I will give you Las Vegas odds that he or she will get the, "Well, this is the way we do things here," speech from the established leaders of that given church!

So, the next time you hear a pastor or fellow believer

say, "God does not give us the spirit of fear," please do not rely on the teachings of your pastor, but show yourself approved by conducting a Greek to English word study so God's truth will be your truth! This statement by Paul to Timothy had a specific message for Timothy and should not be viewed as having a universal and perpetual application. I love what Pastor Jake Gaines says, "Everything in the Bible is for us, but not everything in the Bible was written directly to us." I offer in evidence that 1st and 2nd Timothy are known as two of Paul's "Pastoral Epistles," and an epistle is another word for a letter! First and Second Timothy were letters Paul wrote to his protégé as a means of instruction. Am I making my point?

Earlier, I promised you I would mention some Biblical personages who were afraid. The second chapter of Joshua informs us of the two Israelite spies that Joshua sent into the city of Jericho. These men were hidden by the prostitute, Rahab, who lied to the king of Jericho about the spies' whereabouts at the risk of losing her life. Do you think the two spies and Rahab were afraid?

I Kings 17 enlightens us that God had Ravens bring Elijah sustenance in the form of meat and bread in the morning and evening to keep him alive while he hid out of fear from Ahab, Jezebel, and the pagan priest. God told Elijah to hide in the Kerith ravine from his enemies. Sounds like God feared for the life of His devoted servant, and Elijah did exactly what God told him to do and hid from his enemies!

Let us not forget the plot of the Jews to kill the recently converted to Christianity, Saul/Paul in Acts 9 where his followers had to lower him in a basket through a window so he might escape from being murdered. Paul hid because he had not completed his God-given assignment and because he was afraid!

The greatest biblical story that inarguably illustrates how fear might impact us is found in the synoptic gospels where Jesus, the Son of God, asked the Father, if it was absolutely necessary for Him to endure the scourging or whipping followed by His crucifixion to provide us with salvation. Jesus said, "O My Father, if it be possible, let this cup pass from Me; nevertheless, not as I will, but as Thou wilt. (NIV)"

So, if you have a pastor who teaches you that it is sinful for a Christian to be afraid, you might want to remind him or her that our Lord and Savior was afraid of being scourged and crucified, but His fear did not deter Him from accomplishing His assigned mission on earth. So, if you still feel that God does not give us the spirit of fear as taught by your religious leader, maybe you are a Sucka for a pimp in the pulpit. I am sorry if I sound a little harsh, but our salvation is at stake, so we must know the truth within God's word and not believe without question everything our pastor says. As the Bible states clearly, "Test all things," (I Thessalonians 5:21) including the Biblical interpretations of our religious leaders!

I respectfully suggest to you that God gives us fear to keep us mentally sharp and from being vulnerable in dangerous situations. Gen. Omar N. Bradley brings us clarity on this issue when he said, "Bravery is the capacity to perform properly even when scared half to death."

There is a rule with universal application known as the unity of opposites. It dictates that we need fear so we know and have a well defined appreciation for its opposites: calmness, contentment, confidence, and self-assurance! Enough said?

My second Biblical inaccuracy spawned pet peeve is tithing. Tithing is one of the most abused teachings in the

Christian church of today.

In one of my previous books entitled, *"Show Me The Scripture Because Jim Jones Was A Helluva Preacher Too"* (chapter 7 – Myth of Christian Tithing versus the Truth of Christian Giving), I dedicated an entire chapter to the misnomer that Christians are obligated to tithe. Nothing is farther from the truth. Tithing was part of the Mosaic laws and therefore was only subject to the Jews. There are 613 Mosaic laws, but I find it suspicious that we are exhorted to primarily adhere to or obey the law regarding tithing. When was the last time you had a nice breakfast with bacon or a nice smothered pork chop? Yummy, or blasphemy? But pork, shrimp, lobster (heaven forbid I do love seafood!), and other foods are forbidden under the Mosaic dietary law. I also question why factually, God mandated three tithes under the Mosaic Law, but only one is addressed and taught. Why do some pastors completely ignore the Biblical mandate to pay three tithes which would amount to 20% each year and would leave us with a 30% tithing obligation every third year? We will get to those other tithes as we progress in our discussion.

It is worthy of our attention that every time God gave a command in the Old Testament, he always stated to whom He gave the Law to present to His chosen People. God also generally stated the locale as to where His chosen people were to receive the law and specifically who the recipients were of His Law.

Let us look at the first reference to tithing in Leviticus 27:30-34 in the NIV translation to prove my assertion. [30] "A tithe of everything from the land, whether grain from the soil or fruit from the trees, belongs to the LORD; it is holy to the LORD. [31] Whoever would redeem any of their tithe must add a fifth of the value to it. [32] Every tithe of the herd and flock—every tenth animal that passes under the shepherd's rod—will be holy to the LORD. ³³ No one may pick out the good from the bad or make any substitution. If anyone does make a substitution, both the animal and its substitute become holy and cannot be redeemed. ³⁴ <u>These are the commands the LORD gave Moses at Mount Sinai for the Israelites.</u> But, what bothers me is that there are three tithes God commands in the Mosaic Law, but again, many preachers of today only deal with one, the tithe they make people feel guilty about as they corruptly or incorrectly interpret God's Mosaic Law and tell us that tithing is compulsory for Christians today. If we did not tithe, could some of these millionaire pastors live lavishly? Just something to think about!

Tithing under the Mosaic Law was compulsory only for the Jewish nation and was abolished in the Christian era (CE/AD). Please do not take my word for it. Please consult my previously mentioned book, *"Show Me the Scripture ..."* where you will find that after the second fall and complete destruction of Jerusalem in 70 AD by the Romans, tithing virtually was abolished for almost 500 years. It was not until the reign of Charlemagne that tithes were reinstituted by the Pope. You see, Charlemagne was a devout Roman Catholic and, seeking favor with the Pope, asked the Pope what he could do to expand the Roman Catholic Church. The Pope responded that he had two requirements of Charlemagne. First, he wanted Charlemagne to punish with death if necessary all heretics. Secondly, and more relevant to our discussion, he instructed Charlemagne to inforce and re-institute the practice of tithing so the church could build massive cathedrals throughout Europe or at least the territories controlled by Charlemagne! So tithing, which had virtually had fallen by the wayside and was replaced with generous giving in the Christian era, was reinstituted and, as it is often said, the rest is history!

Please test all things on this topic, and please do not take what I have said at face value. I also may make mistakes, but I know I am not in error on this topic. You will be surprised what you will learn what you do not know about Tithing versus Giving if you do the research I suggested! As a teaser, the book of Malachi says, Bring me all the tithes into the storehouse ... right? But how could the tithes be brought into a storehouse that was destroyed in 70 AD when again the entire city of Jerusalem that housed the storehouse was COMPLETELY DESTROYED?

I assert again that tithing was only compulsory for the Jews, and all we need to do is look at Malachi 1:1 to see who the tithes were mandated for by God, $_1$ The oracle of the word of the LORD to Israel through Malachi. So who was God's messenger and to whom did God's messenger deliver God's Word? Hmm, was God's Words in Malachi addressed to the Egyptians, Babylonians, Assyrians, Chaldeans? No, the tithing messages of Moses and Malachi were only for the ancient Israelites! Question, do we have to obey the laws of Bulgaria if we never go there? So why would I concern myself with any other country's laws, such as their speed limits while I live and remain in the USA? The Jews were obligated to obey the Mosaic Laws, and we are to obey the teachings of Jesus.

The second tithe is known as The "Feast of Tabernacles/Feast of Festival" tithe and is mentioned in Deuteronomy 14:22-27. This was an annual tithe of ten percent and had certain stipulations. Primarily, the tither had to take a tenth of his livestock and / or produce from the field and go to Jerusalem or the nearest religious capitol where he and his entire family would eat the tithe of all they had produced that year and share it with the Levites, the priestly tribe entrusted with the collection of the tithes and maintenance of the temple. It is worthy to note that all tithes collected in all three situations were "foodstuffs" and not money. Please ask your pastor to show you and me the relevant scripture or scriptures where anything other than livestock and / or plants (grains, fruit, cumin, etc.) grown in the field were ever mentioned in the Bible regarding tithing. If the tither was unable to take his tithe for the feast to Jerusalem or the designated place of worship, he was obligated to sell his foodstuff at home and use all the money he received for his produce and purchase food for the festival for himself, his family and the Levites. Please remember there was no refrigeration in the Old Testament era, making it almost impossible to transport food for weeks or more with the expectation they could be consumed at the end of the journey. The object of this second tithe was that Israel should always fear God.

The tither was to eat and rejoice before God. He was also obligated to stay at least a week each at the Passover, Feast of Tabernacles, as well as a briefer period of the Feast of Weeks, which is mentioned in Deuteronomy 16:3, 13, 16. In essence, this second tithe was a tithe of Thanksgiving celebrated by one's entire family to give God glory.

The third tithe was also ten percent but was only collected every three years. It is noteworthy to mention at this juncture, that the three tithes were ONLY collected ONCE annually! This being a Biblical fact, is the collection of tithes and offerings weekly a violation of the Sabbath Laws? Hmm, the Mosaic Sabbath Laws had a death penalty provision for working on Sundays (please see Numbers 15:32-36). Well, I could be wrong, but, is not collecting money more than once a year as mandated by Mosaic Law an act of breaking the Sabbath Laws? Should we take the trustees and deacons out to the parking lot and teach them a lesson they will not forget and stone them to death for breaking God's law? Suitable landscaping stones for stoning are readily available for purchase in the garden department of any home improvement and major hardware store. So, if your pastor teaches tithing as a requirement for today's Christians, should we not follow ALL of God's laws? But, I do digress. Let us return to the third tithe mandated under Mosaic Law. This third tithe, found in Deuteronomy 14:28-29 had a very specific purpose. The Jews subject to the Laws of Moses were obligated to give the Levites ten percent of their annual increase from their harvests of foodstuffs (grains, fruits, etc.) and the increase of their livestock (sheep, cattle etc.). The ancient Jews had storehouses for harvested items since they needed to store foodstuffs until the next harvest. The livestock simply existed in the fields until they were slaughtered for meals. Therefore, the edible items stored at the homes of the Mosaic Jews were used to feed the local Levites, the poor, the destitute, the widows, the strangers/alien travelers, and the fatherless. This tithe was instituted by God so He might bless the Jews for their faithfulness and obedience. May I ask you a question? When was the first time your pastor taught the inherent principles to you and the other members within your congregation concerning the three mandated tithes? When have you gathered your family up and had an annual religious oriented feast to give praise and honor to the Lord? Please do not say, "Well, we do get together each year as a family for Thanksgiving." We all know that while the concept may be similar to the second tithe, the celebration of Thanksgiving in November was spawned by the pilgrims to thank God for their surviving the harsh winters of New England.

My point is simply this, if your pastor teaches tithing, then he is CHEATING, and DISOBEYING God, if he does not mandate you to contribute to all three tithes annually. The absence of the teaching of the whole truth, a known truth, is still a lie!

If tithing were a Godly mandate for Christians, then why did neither, Jesus nor Peter nor Paul nor James nor John write about God's requirement that we tithe?

Please do not get it twisted, I am not saying you do not have to give to the church. Instead, I am saying as Paul wrote, we should give without it being compulsory. We should give cheerfully after deciding what we will give, and we should give generously to the church commensurate to how God has blessed us! So, if your pastor teaches only one tithe, maybe you should suggest that he teaches the truth, the whole truth, and nothing but the truth, about all three tithes. To do otherwise is a gross failure to teach and adhere to the Word of God. Am I right or wrong? We have never been under the Law as Christians. Rather, we have always been under the Lord's Grace and mercy! To run around and brag that you are a tither might subject you to being called a sucka for a pimp in the pulpit! Continue to give to your house of worship commensurate to how God has blessed you!

My third pet peeve stems from this nonsensical doctrine currently being espoused from the pulpit that we must plant a monetary seed in order for the Lord to bless us. It sounds like a "you must pay to play" gospel to me, and it is riddled with inaccuracies. When the scripture says if you sow sparingly, you will reap sparingly, that was yet another of Paul's epistles/letters to a specific audience where he was encouraging the Christian believers to send a financial blessing to support the financially strapped church in Jerusalem. It was a plea similar to that permeating this country today where individuals, organizations, and churches are sending bottled water to the residences of Flint, Michigan! When the emergency has been properly addressed, the water collections for Flint will cease! God's Word is crystal clear on generous giving.

Recently, I was watching a TV evangelist who was supposedly teaching the word of God about fear. So, since that topic is near and dear to my heart, I listened intently to his message. However, this pimp in the pulpit was not talking about being in fear of hell, death, ISIS, Al Qaeda etc., he was teaching that Christians, no matter what their finances, should not be afraid to give their very last dollar to him, excuse me, I meant to the Lord, no matter how dire their financial situation. Honestly, I was angered by this so-called preacher's doctrine and presentation of same. How, I asked, could a preacher say something like, "Even if the County Sherriff is going to set your household goods on the curb on Monday, you need to plant a seed so God will Bless YOU!" Please excuse me, but even as a PK, I cursed this stupid @&%$# (please insert your favorite profane word/words here!) out and even called him a despicable #&%$# (again, please insert your favorite profane word/words here unless you have an unlimited supply, a virtual plethora of profane words.) idiot and the most detestable Maryland Farmer known to man! Again, I apologize, as I lose it every time I think about these $#@ d&%$ con artist.

Please do not get caught up in this nonsense, and I do mean nonsense of planting a monetary seed so God will bless you. On my way to church one Sunday, I was listening to Detroit's excellent Gospel radio station. There was a preacher who said something like, "Well, I have finally convinced my congregation to plant a seed if they are tithers, but I need to get them to understand that they need to plant a major seed for me, their pastor, since I am blessing them." I was outraged! How could a true man of God remotely suggest that not only should his congregants be idiots and give a monetary seed so God will bless them, but they should also plant a monetary seed for this worthless, greedy man allegedly of God!

I am an avid and voracious reader, so I consulted several commentaries to check out what I knew to be an erroneous and distorted teaching of God's Word. I consulted such well known Biblical tools as the Strong's Exhaustive Concordance of the Bible; Bible Commentaries, such as the Life Application New Testament Commentary; the MacArthur Bible Commentary; the Believers Bible Commentary; the granddaddy of all Commentaries, the King James Bible Commentary; the Wycliffe Bible Commentary; and other Biblical research tools. Please let me digress for a moment to make a very important point. There are some pastors who dissuade their congregations from using commentaries, saying that Commentaries are created by man and therefore relegating them to a useless status. I respectfully submit to you that all the Commentaries I mentioned, and they are not all the Commentaries I used, were created by men, extremely Biblically scholarly men. So, if your pastor attempts to get you to negate a Commentary as a Biblical Study tool, please ask him or her what is the difference between a Commentary and their sermons?

After consulting these Biblical tools, I noticed one consistent theme throughout the parable of the Sower or Four Soils has absolutely nothing to do with "planting a monetary seed" to gain favor and be blessed by God. Given all the sources I used, I would like to use the summary of the Commentaries related to the proper interpretation of the parable of the sower or the Parable of the Four Soils located in the synoptic Gospels presented by the Christian website, gotquestions.org.

The gotquestions.org analysis and proper interpretation of the relevant scripture reads thusly, "The

Parable of the Sower concerns a sower who scatters seed, which falls on four different types of ground. The hard ground "by the way side" prevents the seed from sprouting at all, and the seed becomes nothing more than bird food. The stony ground provides enough soil for the seeds to germinate and begin to grow, but because there is "no deepness of earth," the plants do not take root and are soon withered in the sun. The thorny ground allows the seed to grow, but the competing thorns choke the life out of the beneficial plants. The good ground receives the seed and produces much fruit.

Jesus' explanation of the Parable of the Sower highlights four different responses to the gospel. The seed is "the word of the kingdom." The hard ground represents someone who is hardened by sin; he hears but does not understand the Word, and Satan plucks the message away, keeping the heart dull and preventing the Word from making an impression. The stony ground pictures a man who professes delight with the Word; however, his heart is not changed, and when trouble arises, his so-called faith quickly disappears. The thorny ground depicts one who seems to receive the Word, but whose heart is full of <u>riches</u>, <u>pleasures</u>, and <u>lusts</u>; the things of this world take his time and attention away from the Word, and he ends up having no time for it. The good ground portrays the one who hears, understands, and receives the Word—and then allows the Word to accomplish its result in his life. The man represented by the "good ground" is the only one of the four who is truly saved, because salvation's proof is fruit (<u>Matthew 3:7-8</u>; <u>7:15-20</u>).

To summarize the point of the Parable of the Sower: "A man's reception of God's Word is determined by the condition of his heart." A secondary lesson would be "Salvation is more than a superficial, albeit joyful, hearing of the gospel. Someone who is truly saved will go on to prove it."

May our faith and our lives exemplify the "good soil" in the Parable of the Sower."

My Sisters and Brothers in Christ, if you are being taught a distorted gospel, please LEARN to DISCERN God's Word for yourself! The seed addressed in the parable of the Sower or the Four Soils is not a monetary seed but a Spiritual Seed planted in our hearts by our Lord and Savior Jesus Christ. The words of Dr. Joseph Goebbels, Hitler's Minister of Propaganda, are worthy of being repeated here, "Repeat a Lie a thousand times and it will become the truth!" Please do not allow the lies of the prosperity gospel, especially its most abused theme of planting a monetary seed to gain favor with the Lord, become one of your Biblical truths. Pastors who teach this false gospel are only seeking to make money off your lack of knowledge of God's Divine message for you: not to love any other imagined god before Him, to love your neighbor as you love yourself, and to help spread the Gospel of Jesus Christ every day and every way you can!

One can look at Paul's discussion of the scripture regarding the "double honor" paid to preachers that is also being distorted in the manner that it is being taught by these pimps in the pulpit. Paul used the oxen in his example. Hmm! Oxen are beasts of burden that Paul clearly suggests were not the greatest concern of God; rather, God was concerned with the spreading of the Gospel! But, these pimps in the pulpit want us to think they should receive exorbitant salaries, or double pay because they are skillful in interpreting God's Word for us. Do you remember that adage, "A fool and his money will soon be parted"?

I am reminded of the words of Vivian Leigh's character, Blanche Dubois, in the movie, *"A Streetcar Named Desire!"* Blanche Dubois said with tremendous emphasis, "I have always depended on the kindness of strangers."

Jesus and His Disciples all depended on the kindness of friends and strangers. They never sought a fabulous home, an expensive chariot, never had a valet, fine clothes, wealth, status, or what the world purports to be power. No, they sought the means of maintaining and sustaining one another, so they might build God's kingdom here on earth. But, what I too often see are these greedy, shameful, deceptive brokers of the distorted gospels of prosperity, name it and claim it, and let me not forget the most despicable, plant a seed gospel.

Please do not ask me if I think preachers should be millionaires because my response will be, Hell NO! Please do not ask me if preachers should live better than the masses of the people in their congregations because again my retort will be a resounding, Hell NO!

Jesus was a carpenter. Peter, his brother, Andrew, James, and John, were all fishermen. Matthew was a tax collector, a despised profession of his day. Luke was a physician, and the Apostle Paul was a tent maker. What do all these men have in common? Well, they played a major role in the foundation and establishment of the Christian church. In addition, they were all gifted preachers of the gospel of Jesus Christ. Further, they all lived a meager existence, or as it is often said, they lived from pillar to post. However, what is awe-inspiring to me is that they all opted NOT to live the lifestyle of the rich and famous of their day. They worked for their living! I think it's important at this point to remind you of one undeniable fact that I have asserted in other articles in this book: I do not Hate All Preachers! I just despise, detest, and reject those preachers who use and abuse God's word to make an extraordinarily good living. Why cannot your pastor and my pastor be like the Apostle Paul when he wrote in I Corinthians 9:14-18, [14] In the same way, the Lord has commanded that those who preach the gospel should receive their living from the gospel. ¹⁵ But I have not used any of these rights. And I am not writing this in the hope that you will do such things for me, for I would rather DIE than allow anyone to deprive me of this boast. ¹⁶ For when I preach the gospel, I cannot boast, since I am compelled to preach. Woe to me if I do not preach the gospel! ¹⁷ If I preach voluntarily, I have a reward; if not voluntarily, I am simply discharging the trust committed to me.¹⁸ What then is my reward? Just this: that in preaching the gospel I may offer it FREE OF CHARGE, and so not make full use of my rights as a preacher of the gospel.

There are some Christians who will say I am a Hater, but nothing is farther from the truth. You see, I can read! I can also discern fact from fiction, and most importantly, I know that the scriptures talk about false prophets and false teachers. The world abounds with false prophets, preachers, and teachers, and the sad commentary is that too many professed Christians have placed their salvation and eternal lives in the hands of what I incessantly refer to as pimps in the pulpit!

You may believe that your pastor is special in your eyes, an anointed man or woman of God, but if they are teaching you the distorted gospel of buying your way into heaven, your assessment is way off center. If your pastor eats better and more often than you, dresses much better than you, lives in a better home than you, and drives a much more expensive automobile, maybe you are a dupe who does not study God's Word in earnest and is placing your salvation at risk!

Your pastor, elder, bishop, apostle etc., may be great in your eyes, but is he or she great in the eyes of almighty God?

Brother James

I sincerely pray this book has been a blessing to you, and more importantly, I sincerely pray that the Controversial Interrogatories contained within this book made you think!

ARTICLE 23

Do You Want and Need a God You Can See?

Idolatry, the worship of a physical object as a god, is the greatest sin! The book of Exodus clearly informs us that God hates idolatry; therefore, He hates idol worshippers! Exodus 20:3-6 states, "³ You shall have no other gods before me. ⁴ You shall not make for yourself an image in the form of anything in heaven above or on the earth, beneath or in the waters below. ⁵ You shall not bow down to them or worship them; for I, the LORD your God, am a jealous God, punishing the children for the sin of the parents to the third and fourth generation of those who hate me, ⁶ but showing love to a thousand generations of those who love me and keep my commandments." It is evident from this block of scripture that there is only one Almighty God and that He is worthy of our most sincere praise and worship. But, what brought about idolatry in ancient societies, and does idolatry exists today?

So we may be clear, let us look at the dictionary definition of idolatry. The Merriam-Webster's dictionary defines idolatry in the following way, "Idolatry is the worship of an idol or a physical object as a representation of a god; an immoderate (exceeding just, usual, or suitable bounds) attachment or devotion to something." Wikipedia.com further explores the definition of idolatry when it states, "In all the Abrahamic religions idolatry is strongly forbidden, ... Behavior considered idolatrous or potentially idolatrous may include the creation of any type of image of the deity, or of other figures of religious significance such as <u>prophets, saints, and <u>CLERGY</u>,...</u>" Hmm, the CLERGY! Are there those who make idols of their pastor?

Many ancient societies were idol worshippers because they made an image of what they perceived to be god or a demon/devil out of wood, stone, or molten metals etc. But, why did early people create what the Bible calls graven images?

Members of ancient societies were witnesses to Almighty God's marvelous creations on earth, the solar system, and each other. These ancient societies made images of gods and demons to explain what they experienced and could not explain in their lives. Some primitive societies had a specific god for the sun, rain, seasons, waterways in their nations, etc. In essence, there were gods for every unexplained phenomenon in the environments of primitive societies. This idolatry is known as polytheism, the belief in multiple gods. If we were to look at the powerful nation of ancient Egypt, there were at least 29 gods that they made images and paintings of in their worship system. The Egyptians' most important god was Ra, the Sun god. It was believed that Ra awoke in the morning, illuminated the earth, and then was swallowed by Nut, the Night goddess. Each morning Ra was reborn, and this day and night cycle between Ra and Nut would occur each and every day and night. Other Egyptian idol gods were, Ma' at; the goddess of truth, justice, and harmony; Ptah, the god of the craftsmen; Sobek, god of the Nile river; Shu, the god of the air; Sekhmet, the goddess of war; Seth, the god of chaos; and Osiris, the god of the underworld (the place where everyone would be judged and would be subjected to a series of tests to determine if they would be granted everlasting life), the dead, and resurrection. So, we may assume that the ancient Egyptians, much like many of their contemporaries, needed someone to whom they could and should attribute these magnificent creations and miracles in their lives. They wanted and needed a god or gods they could see!

Interestingly, it was the Egyptian Pharaoh, Akhenatan (1352-1336 BC), who became known as the heretic Pharaoh because he introduced the belief in one god (monotheism). A careful review of the Egyptian Book of the Dead in the Papyrus of Ani, a book of Egyptian civil/judicial, moral, and ceremonial laws, would show us similarities to the Mosaic Laws. Contained within the Egyptian Book of the Dead is the 42 Negative Confessions. A serious and careful review of the 42 Negative Confessions would show us similarities to the 10 Commandments. For example, Negative Confessions 2-3 state, (2) I have not committed robbery with violence. (3) I have not stolen (thou shall not steal). Negative Confessions 4, 12, and 18 respectively read (4) I have not slain men and women (thou shall not kill), (12) I have not committed adultery (thou shall not commit adultery), (18) I have slandered [no man] (thou shall not bear false witness against thy neighbor). These Negative Confessions, written about 2000 years before the birth of Moses, clearly illustrate that Almighty God spoke to all the people of the ancient world, even though they may have been idolaters!

Knowing the aforementioned background related to idolatry, are you an idol worshipper? Do you worship at the altar of money, status, power, and perceived entitled privilege, or, even worse, do you worship some alleged man or woman of the cloth who espouses the sinful gospels of "prosperity," "name it and claim it," and the "plant a seed to be blessed by God" gospel? The Apostle Paul informs us in Galatians 1:6-12, that there is but one gospel, the gospel of Jesus Christ. The NIV translation of this scripture reads, "[6] I am astonished that you are so quickly deserting the one who called you to live in the grace of Christ and are turning to a different gospel—⁷ which is really no gospel at all. Evidently some people are throwing you into confusion and are trying to pervert the gospel of Christ. ⁸ But even if we or an angel from heaven should preach a gospel other than the one we preached to you, let them be under God's curse! ⁹ As we have already said, so now I say again: If anybody is preaching to you a gospel other than what you accepted, let them be under God's curse! ¹⁰ Am I now trying to win the approval of human beings, or of God? Or am I trying to please people? If I were still trying to please people, I would not be a servant of Christ."

Are you truly a devotee of Jesus, whom you cannot see, or, are you opting to place all your faith in a man or woman in the pulpit whom you can see? Too many professed Christian folk are opting to make their pastor a god on earth and make blasphemous statements that begin with, "My pastor said," instead of prefacing their insightful religious remarks by saying, "The Word of God says." I mentioned earlier in this discourse that ancient societies had to have a god they could see. Hence, the creation of idol gods. I respectfully submit to you that idolatry exists in this modern era because people want and need a god they can see, and their idol is someone to whom they attribute the powers, grace, and mercy only attainable through Jesus Christ. This form of idolatry is becoming widespread as it was predicted/prophesied in the New Testament.

When I reflect upon those who claim to be Christians but are making an idol of their pastor, I cannot help but think of the lyrics of the song performed by the Motown group, the Temptations, *"I want a love I can see."* Let us look at the first stanza of these lyrics to further our discussion.

Is God Fair

"I want a love I can see. That's the only kind that means a thing to me. Don't want a love you have to tell me about. That kind of loving I can sure do without."

Now, if we were to replace the words LOVE and LOVING in these lyrics with the word, god, we would get the following message that substantiates my posture that some professed Christians are idol worshippers!

I want a god I can see. That's the only kind that means a thing to me. Don't want a god you have to tell me about. That kind of god I can sure do without.

So, I respectfully ask again, do you want and need a god you can see (in the pulpit), or can you willingly submit to and believe in a God you will see in heaven? This is a very serious question that is worthy of deliberate consideration. Please believe in Almighty God whom you cannot see, as opposed to some person driving an expensive car, who lives in an exclusive neighborhood, and is the only person in your congregation prospering from <u>the fruit of your and others labor</u>!

There are, in my opinion, two distinctly different types of preachers: sincere or insincere! Please find and join a congregation where the pastor is widely known for his/her good works.

Yes, I want a God I can see, but, I am willing to wait to see Him in heaven. I am, by no means an idol worshiper of any pastor! How about you?

EPILOGUE

I do not question the word of Almighty God, but I do reserve the right to question how it is being taught and applied! Please learn to discern the Word of Almighty God in its quintessential essence and form!

– Brother James –

I mentioned earlier that Dr. Joseph Goebbels, Hitler's Minister of Propaganda, stated "Repeat a lie a thousand times and it becomes the truth!"

A few years ago at the close of a course on Biblical Hermeneutics, Pastor Jake Gaines, Pastor of Synagogue Baptist Church, Detroit, and an outstanding facilitator and teacher of God's word, posed the question, "What is the most important lesson you will take away from this course?" When it was my turn to respond, I said, "I have learned what I must unlearn about the Word of God because I must now look at how some of what I thought to be true is not true!"

Respectfully, I warned you from the outset that as an avid reader and researcher of God's Word, I am very opinionated! I sincerely pray that you found this work thought provoking and inspirational enough that you aspire to show yourself approved by doing some in-depth Biblical research.

I am reminded at this juncture of an African fable,

"The Tortoise and the Birds" that I will use literary license with in order that I might adroitly speak to the prevailing issue of this book: You must learn to understand God's Word for YOURSELF!

My rendition of the African fable of "The Tortoise and the Birds" goes something like this.

One day God decided to call the pastor and ALL the congregants of a mega church to heaven so He might speak to and bless them. God wanted them to study to show themselves approved as diligent workers in His earthly vineyard. The Pastor of the church, Pastor I. M. Everso Greedy, when hearing God's invitation, held a meeting and told the massive throng of congregants, "Since I am the pastor, the most sophisticated, the most eloquent and articulate of ALL the people in the church, please allow me to be the spokesperson for ALL of us. And I suggest that when we meet God, that you ALL will agree to address me as ALL OF YOU instead of pastor! So, when we meet Almighty God, He too will address me as ALL OF YOU since I am the designated leader. ...."

The entire congregation, trusting their pastor whom they viewed as a god, were a little puzzled about his request, but agreed. Shortly after the meeting, the pastor and the congregation were swept up into heaven. After welcoming them, God said, I have prepared a sumptuous feast for ALL OF YOU.

I have prepared these beautiful mansions for ALL OF YOU! I have eliminated sickness, poverty, and inequality and will provide ALL OF YOU with a pain-free existence forever! I will accommodate ALL OF YOU with All the desires of your heart! And, I will extend eternal life to ALL OF YOU!

God then left their company to attend to other business. Pastor Greedy, then said proudly, "Do you see how God loves me more than any of you? Do you see how He has blessed me more than any of you? Do you see how God has elevated me to a status where my authority should never be questioned? God gave me everything because everything He presented to us He clearly said was for me, ALL OF YOU! So, I want each of you to bow down to me as a god second only to Almighty God because you All heard God when He said all these things are for ALL OF YOU!" Instead of questioning Pastor Greedy, the entire congregation began to sheepishly serve him unquestionably thereafter and did so for the rest of their lives, completely missing out on ALL the blessings God had in store for and had promised them!

Can a man or woman rob God? Yes, they can! They can rob God of the credit He is due by taking credit for God's good works. Have you heard pastors say they healed people or, they built this church? Yes, a man or woman can rob God, and we do not realize it!

I pray you got my message as too many people think they are going to heaven, but they are being led astray! Attending some churches led by greedy and unscrupulous pastors is akin to taking small but incremental daily doses of arsenic. Arsenic in miniscule quantities is in the air we breathe, the water we drink, and the ground from which our vegetables and fruits emanate. We have a very small amount of arsenic in our bodies, and as long as we do not exceed our personal threshold of arsenic, we will be okay. However, once our arsenic levels are increased by someone intent on destroying us, we will surely perish. My analogy suggests that if we take in the arsenic of the distorted gospels of these false teachers, these pimps in the pulpit, we will surely die spiritually!

Is God Fair

I pray that you have a personal relationship with the Lord and will not have a problem entering the gates of heaven. I envision entering heaven as akin to entering into a foreign country. To enter a foreign country, you must have a valid passport as proof of who you are. Your valid passport entitles you to enter the foreign country just as your good Christian works will serve as your valid passport to enter heaven. I also envision the gates of heaven as being like going through Customs where your personal effects are checked to insure you are not bringing any contraband items, such as sin along. I also see inclusive in this Customs-like process long lines, and people being denied entry into a foreign country because their identification is not sufficient or not in order. When I have travelled outside this country, I have experienced some extensive questioning by the Customs officials, but when I proved who I said I was, I was granted <u>admittance.</u>

Heaven is like another country, a utopian society of Love, one for the other. There will be no greed, envy, hatred or any other societal negatives there. There will be no crime, poverty, sickness, inequality, etc. Will you have a valid passport to enter heaven? Will you attempt to bring in some contraband? Or, will Peter greet you at the pearly gates and introduce you to Jesus, who will embrace you and say, "Well done my good and faithful Servant!"

Jesus said in Matthew 7:21 (NIV) "Not everyone who says to me, 'Lord, Lord,' will enter the kingdom of heaven, but only the one who does the will of my Father who is in heaven.

I sincerely pray that you attend a truly Bible based teaching church in your community. Be Blessed, and again, please learn to discern the Word of God for yourself!

CREDITS

INSPIRATION   God the Father, Jesus the Son, The Holy Spirit
                                          My parents

EDITOR   Ray Glandon
BOOK COVER CONCEPT FRONT
AND BACK   Brother James
Back Cover Artwork   Tim James

www.ingramcontent.com/pod-product-compliance
Lightning Source LLC
Chambersburg PA
CBHW070639050426
42451CB00008B/227